TRADING PLACES
EUROPE'S FINEST SPECIALIST SHOPS

TRADING PLACES
EUROPE'S FINEST SPECIALIST SHOPS

HATTIE ELLIS

PHOTOGRAPHS BY JILL MEAD

MITCHELL BEAZLEY

TRADING PLACES
by Hattie Ellis

First published in Great Britain in 2000 by Mitchell Beazley,
an imprint of the Octopus Publishing Group Ltd,
2–4 Heron Quays, London E14 4JB

ISBN 1 84000 256 5

A CIP catalogue record for this book is available
from the British Library

Commissioning Editor: Margaret Little
Art Director: Rita Wuthrich
Executive Art Editor: Tracy Killick
Design: Lovelock & Co
Editor: Stephen Guise
Production: Nancy Roberts

Typeset in Goudy
Printed and bound by Toppan in China

CONTENTS

INTRODUCTION

Shopping is a revealing, entertaining and yet frequently overlooked part of travel. Guidebooks devote pages to buildings and art galleries but barely mention the charismatic specialist shops. Why not? Set up to cater for the needs and desires of a particular community, they take you right to the heart of a place, into the living culture that is so interesting to encounter and yet often so elusive.

In the same way that you might seek out a good restaurant or museum, all the specialist shops in this book are worth a detour. The bicycle inventor (T'Mannetje), the 18th-century herbalist (Jacob Hooy) and the counterculture comic store (Lambiek) are as much a part of Amsterdam as the canal life and the elegantly wonky old buildings. You can join the Parisians who queue for the world-famous bread at Poilâne's; seek out buttons at Knopf Paul in Berlin along with the professional designers who know its treasures; stroll with an ice-cream at midnight from the Gelateria San Crispino in Rome; or catch a whiff of eccentricity at Smith's, the excellent umbrella shop in London. Specialist shops are open doorways onto enticing new worlds.

Unlike the shuffling 'morgues' of modern retail, where piped muzak and ringing tills are the only sounds, these shops are alive with incident, conversations and characters. Deyrolle, a natural history and taxidermy shop in Paris, is perhaps the most eccentric – a parquet-floored zoo of stuffed animals where you may see a polar bear with its fur dyed pink – but all the shops in this book are entertaining once you regard them as places for more than just purchases. Some have an old-world charm, such as Casa Crespo, an espadrille shop in Madrid with floorboards ridged by decades of returning customers. Others are quirky, such as Robert Mills in Bristol, where you can buy bits of old churches and shops; or Plasten, a shop specializing in '50s, '60s and '70s plastic; or Casa Antigua, where the assiduous shopkeeper watches over his breakable stock. Many are real sensual treats: the chic concoctions of Wittamer's *pâtisserie* in Brussels; the crackle and scent of toasted nuts in Gispert, Barcelona; Marianne's shellfish deli in Stokholm, where the counter is a crustacean still-life 'to go'; the jars of pure pigment in Cornelissen, an artists' suppliers in London; and the scented wisps of blue smoke in the marble and leather interior of P C J Hajenius, a beautiful cigar shop in Amsterdam.

Others cross boundaries and are fired by the energy and spirit of creative minds. Larch Cottage, an exceptional garden nursery in the Lake District, also produces wood-fired pizzas, cakes and stained glass. Rosendals Trädgard, a biodynamic pleasure garden in Stokholm, is principally a place to *be* rather than a strictly commercial concern.

What goes on behind the counters is often dynamic. A shop may retain an old-fashioned appearance and sense of personal service, but you soon learn that it only survives through Olympian endeavour and by never ceasing to change. Sometimes the stories are poignant: of exile and sacrifice, or of the difficulty of maintaining quality in a hurried world. Occasionally it is clear that the future hangs by the fine thread of an individual's commitment or a family's sense of tradition. Some of the shopkeepers have given up other careers to follow their parents. Will another generation be so dutiful?

We have a part to play, too, in the survival of these exceptional 'trading places'. As consumer patrons, we can vote with our cash to enjoy, and sustain, the best. The specialist shop offers an inspired individuality, a commitment to quality and an extraordinary level of expertise that is all at your service, just a step off the street.

VALVONA & CROLLA

Delicatessen

FOUNDED *Early 1860s by Benedetto Valvona; Alfonsa Crolla joined in 1934*

OWNERS *The Continis (Alfonsa's grandchildren)*

SPECIALITIES *Italian food, including imports of fresh fruit and vegetables from Milan's produce market; home-made breads; malt whisky; outstanding Italian wine list*

ADDRESS/PHONE *19 Elm Row, Edinburgh EH7 4AA; tel: 0131 556 6066, fax: 0131 556 1668*

E-MAIL/INTERNET *sales@valvonacrolla.co.uk www.valvonacrolla.co.uk*

NEAR *A ten-minute walk from Waverley Station and the east end of Princes Street; Elm Row is part of Leith Walk*

MAIL ORDER *The shop produces a wine and whisky list; see also the Internet site*

OPENING HOURS *Monday to Wednesday 8am–6pm; Thursday and Friday 8am–7.30pm; Saturday 8am–6pm*

Whatever the Edinburgh skies, this shop brings sunlight to the senses. The front room is a canyon of shelves 11-storeys high. Layers of ham and dried peppers tumble down from above, rock salt sparkles on the *ciabatta* and Italian songs lighten your step.

Passed down the generations, the shop is run by two brothers, Philip and Victor Contini, and their wives, Mary and Carina, who are sisters. Both families are originally from southern Italy, where the sun makes good food abundant, delicious and cheap.

There is nothing precious about Valvona & Crolla: just a down-to-earth yet operatic sense of pleasure. When they began importing from Milan's produce market, some Italian locals wept for joy at the arrival of the first Sardinian tomatoes, Neapolitan figs and sweet, white-fleshed peaches. The business started life as a wholesaler in the Grassmarket, where Italian immigrants gathered in Edinburgh's equivalent of a piazza. It was after moving to Leith Walk that Valvona & Crolla became well loved. It was run for decades by Victor Crolla, a famous Edinburgh character: customers came in for the patter as well as the *antipasti*. At times the long, narrow room got so crowded that goods had to be thrown along the counter, over the heads of the servers. One day a flying bag of turmeric caught on a salami hook and showered the shop in deep yellow.

Philip Contini, Victor Crolla's nephew, is fascinated by wine, and the shop's list of Italian wines has been called the best in Britain. Some are served by the glass at the shop's *caffè*-bar, or you can pick a bottle from the shelves to drink with a plate of very good food for a corkage charge of £3 per bottle. The first bottles

you see when you walk in the door, however, are the single malt whiskies. Philip says two Scots will quietly bond over a dram in the same way as Southern Italians might over a plate of pasta.

At every other step there is a personal connection between family and friends. The wine room fittings were made, without a nail, by a relative in Naples. A freezer cabinet contains one kind of ice-cream made by a neighbour, another by a friend and a third that reminds Mary of those made by her own family. She eats Italian ice-cream every day.

The tight-knit nature of the Scottish-Italian community has led in

Left The policy is to encourage customers to taste the foods – hence sample slivers are handed to people waiting in line at the shop's long counter.

Below The products are imported directly from family, contacts and friends. Lorry-loads of fresh fruit and vegetables arrive twice a week from Milan's produce market.

the past to parallel tragedies. Both the Continis and Mary's and Carina's family, the Di Ciaccas, lost grandfathers when a boat carrying interned Italians to Canada was torpedoed during the Second World War. The night that Mussolini declared war, there were anti-Italian riots in Leith Walk. You wouldn't guess to look, but boards put up to protect the shop still form part of its frontage: a sombre reminder of darker years.

Left *Eleven storeys of shelves and an additional room at the back of the shop hold an outstanding selection of Italian wines – around 1,000 kinds in all.*

Below *Tomatoes that have been ripened by the Southern Italian sun: full of sweetness and flavour. Taste counts for everything at Valvona & Crolla.*

E & A GISPERT

Toasted nuts & dried fruit

FOUNDED *1851 by Enric and Alfonso Gispert*
OWNERS *Cisçu and Ricard Hargenat*
SPECIALITIES *Toasted nuts, dried fruits and spices*
ADDRESS/PHONE *Sombrerers 23, Barri de la Ribera, 08003 Barcelona, Spain; tel: (00 34) 93 319 7535, fax: (00 34) 93 319 7171*
E-MAIL *gispert@vilaweb.com*
NEAR *Santa María del Mar, metro Jaume 1, the Picasso Museum*
OPENING HOURS *Monday to Friday 9am–1.30pm, 4pm–7.30pm; Saturday 10am–2pm, 5pm–8pm*

During the winter people come into Gispert's for nuts still warm from the wood-fired oven and eat them walking down the street with their hands cupped around the fragrant, toasty bags. The almonds and hazelnuts taste slightly smoky; the odd crackle can be heard from the depths of the big baskets in the shop, not unlike the sound of sparking embers.

Catalonia is famous for its nuts, especially those from Tarragona further down the coast. Nuts appear everywhere in the glittering windows of Barcelona cake shops, as shards of toasted almonds on sugar-coated sponges, or in the form of pine-nuts – 'the caviar of the forest' – scattered across tarts. Nuts, in a mixture known as a *picada*, also thicken and flavour many savoury Catalan dishes.

The best time to visit this shop is from September and October, when the new nut harvest arrives, through to spring. Don't miss the rich, buttery marcona almonds. Once the local produce runs out, Gispert stocks up with imports, maintaining a great range of nuts, dried fruits, spices and Catalan olive oil as well as such summery delights as almond crackle ice-cream.

Nothing much has changed since the shop opened in 1851. About 60 years ago a motor was fitted to rotate the drum in the oven in which the nuts are roasted. They like to roast plenty of nuts in winter to keep the building warm. The piles of nuts and dried fruits have rich, glistening colours – browns, oranges, reds and blacks – like varnished Old Master paintings. At the back, a tabletop display shows off their textures and colours: ridged pecans and rolling hazelnuts; opaque jewels of dried papaya and the gloss of a walnut shell; tough Brazils and white curls of coconut.

Left *The narrow twisting streets in the Gothic quarter of Barcelona hold gems such as Gispert, where the scent of freshly toasted nuts beckons you through the door.*

Right *Nuts are roasted in a wood-fired oven and sifted in front of a fan so that they are blown clean before being placed, still warm, in big baskets.*

LIONEL POILANE

Bread

FOUNDED *1932 by Pierre Poilâne*

OWNER *Lionel Poilâne, Pierre's son*

SPECIALITIES *Big, round sourdough loaves, raisin bread, apple tarts*

ADDRESS/PHONE *8 rue du Cherche-Midi, 75006 Paris, France; tel: (00 331) 4548 4259, fax: (00 331) 4544 9980*

E-MAIL/INTERNET *commerce@poilane.fr www.poilane.fr*

NEAR *Metro St-Sulpice*

MAIL ORDER *Loaves are delivered by Federal Express, but are also available in good delicatessens and a London branch of Poilâne at 46 Elizabeth Street, London SW1*

OPENING HOURS *Monday to Saturday 7.15am–8.15pm*

The world's most famous bakery is so small that ten customers make a crowd. At weekends, there may well be a queue snaking down the street outside. In the 1970s, a Soviet newspaper showed a photograph of this long line as evidence of Western deprivation.

People queue for a sourdough loaf that has an honest chew and gives a profound sense of pleasure. The apple tarts are a treat for all the senses. Each one has a caramelized centre and pastry that produces an elegant crackle at first bite and the finest flutter of buttery flakes to your sweet, sticky lips.

Lionel Poilâne says his innovation was simple: not to change the recipes at all.

Left *This reception room, visible from the front of the shop, is lit by a dough candelabra Lionel Poilâne made for Salvador Dali. Some of the paintings on the wall are by impoverished Left-bank artists, who painted Poilâne's famous loaves in exchange for bread during the hungry years of the Second World War.*

Above *An assistant works in the bakery below the shop. Every single employee is continuously trained with wide-ranging lessons on all aspects of bread and bread-baking, including culture, history and biology, as well as the techniques and ingredients.*

On this principle he has built a business that supplies two and a half per cent of all Paris' bread, and his fame has spread among food-lovers worldwide. Five thousand customers in America get their *pain Poilâne* by Federal Express.

One of the first things Lionel did on taking over from his father in 1965 was to get rid of the baguettes, those 19th-century interlopers to the French tradition, which his father had made reluctantly. Instead, he concentrated on the traditional, round sourdough loaves.

Poilâne's stands apart from standard bakeries in other ways; the firm does not, for example, employ anyone who has worked in an inferior *boulangerie* and learned bad habits. Employees train in a CD ROM box in the back of the shop that has 120 ten-minute lessons ranging over culture, hygiene and history as well as details about the ingredients of bread, from the wheat to the salt.

Perhaps most unusual of all, the business has managed to expand without losing an ethos of quality and craft. Lionel is a passionate advocate of the artisan, believing the hand to be the finest of instruments. In the bakery below the shop and the purpose-built *manufacture* 14.5km (9 miles) south of Paris, the kneading of the dough may be

done by machine, but the water is added by hand because the amount varies according to the flour and the humidity on the day. Lionel is no Luddite about new technology but he does believe that the automated baker loses touch with the craft and easily becomes a bad baker.

Beneath the Paris shop is a hot cellar where I watched a baker reach into a container of dough that had a slow, thick, sexy wobble. He broke off pieces and put them in cloth-lined wicker baskets. In a wood-fired bread oven, an ashy glow illuminated the shapes of rolls and loaves.

Lionel followed his father into this underground world at the age of 14, to work 12 hours a day, six days a week. He hated it. Friends went off to travel and to study. It took some time before the younger Poilâne realized that bread put the world at his fingertips: art, philosophy, economics, biology, history,

gastronomy. Bread proved to be the best school in the end, he says.

Aged 22, the young baker met Salvador Dali and made bread furniture and picture frames for him. A dough chandelier can be seen behind the shop counter, in a room that is more or less covered in paintings that Lionel's father received in payment for the bread he gave to hungry artists during the war.

He then spent two years going around 10,000 bakeries discovering 81 different kinds of bread, making a map of France's wealth of loaves (many of which are now extinct). The shop's paper bags celebrate 12 people from the history of the world who have been important to bread and baking.

Lionel's principle of taking the best of the old and the new is summed up in his phrase 'retro-innovation'. He quotes from Nietzsche: 'The man of the future is the one with the longest memory.'

Right *Bags of Poilâne's little biscuits. These sweet morsels may be offered to people waiting in line outside the tiny, world-famous bakery.*

Left *The famous pain Poilâne, a big sourdough loaf that is the Parisienne cook's secret weapon because it tastes delicious and stays fresh longer than a baguette.*

Below *The wood-fired oven in Poilâne's produces a high, dry heat that is perfect for baking bread.*

MARIANNE'S FISK OCH DELIKATESSEN

Delicatessen

FOUNDED *1906*

OWNER *Marianne Söderberg*

SPECIALITIES *Shellfish, fish, home-cured herrings, home-made sauces, fine Swedish foods*

ADDRESS/PHONE *Karlbergsvägen 67, Stockholm, Sweden; tel/fax: (00 46) 8 30 10 71*

NEAR *Bus route 47 on Vasastan island; Plasten plastic shop (see pages 78–79)*

OPENING HOURS *Monday to Friday 10am–6pm; Saturday 10am–2pm*

Marianne Söderberg changes her earrings – 23 pairs – with the seasons: crayfish in August, then crabs and then lobsters. Prawns and salmon are more permanent fixtures. She cures herrings (the fish, not the earrings) in 12 ways to celebrate Christmas and midsummer. Then there are the notorious *surstromming*, or sour herrings, which are fermented and kept in tins that bulge slightly with gas. They are eaten with great ceremony (and potatoes). Yet it is not something you would leave open in the fridge, and I doubt that even Marianne dangles a pair of mini-pots from her ears.

Seasons are extreme in Sweden and the festivals suitably heart-felt. Crayfish feasts epitomize summer holiday freedom, with parties all over the country as children haul in the catch from the local lake at first light.

Above *Marianne Söderberg used to spend summers cooking on ships, until she came home to berth in this old-fashioned shellfish deli full of home-made produce and sparkling fish.*

The bounty is then cooked and eaten with special songs and 'an aquavit for every claw'.

Marianne cooks her crayfish traditionally: in salt water with beer and dill flower heads. On the day I visited, she had already prepared 4,000 for the weekend. Wonderful scents danced through the kitchen door and the jovial activity escalated when an assistant slipped and a boxful of crayfish tried to scuttle away like big, clattery spiders.

On Fridays, the counter is a still-life to go. People leave work and buy shellfish to eat without further ado; fish they tend to cook, with more leisure, at the weekends. Customers cross the city to come here, and Marianne strives to maintain high standards so that no one is disappointed. The prawn buyer picks the sweetest in the market; Marianne favours plump Norwegian crabs and the wild Baltic salmon that have pale-pink flesh (which one customer described as 'the colour of grandmothers' knickers'). The crispbread is subtly lactic.

The principle of excellence is crucial with shellfish, which, at their best, have a magnificent succulence; anything less is a dissolute fall from grace. Here you feast with the gods.

Below *Home-made gravadlax and salmon pudding made with salted salmon and raisins are two traditional Swedish dishes on sale at the shop. More and more people want ultra-fresh fish to make sushi and sashimi.*

Above *Customers come in for single fish or shellfish feasts. One had just ordered 1,600 crayfish for a traditional summer guzzle, an annual event that is accompanied by songs and aquavits.*

PFUND'S MOLKEREI

Cheese

FOUNDED *1880 by Paul Pfund*

OWNER *Baufinanz in Sachsen*

SPECIALITIES *Unpasteurised cheeses and local wines*

ADDRESS/PHONE *Bautzner Strasse 79, 01099 Dresden, Germany; tel:(00 49) 351 808080, fax:(00 49) 351 8080820*

E-MAIL/INTERNET *Pfunds.Molkerei@gmx.de www.pfunds.de*

NEAR *Neustadt district of Dresden*

OPENING HOURS *Monday to Saturday 9am–8pm; Sunday 10am–4pm*

This is a strikingly pretty shop, filled with the sweet nursery innocence of milk. Purity was at the heart of the Pfund empire that rose to prominence at the end of the 19th century. The founder, Paul Pfund, came to Dresden at a time when milk was being brought into the city from the countryside in open, unhygienic carts – with fatal results. His innovation was to bring the cows into the city and milk them in front of the customers, filtering the milk through fine cloths.

These rooms were a showcase for the business. Saxony has had plenty of kings and aristocrats who planned vast castles that were never finished; Paul Pfund created 70 square metres of perfection.

Left *One of the
prettiest shops in
Europe, Pfund's was
the showcase of an
empire established
by a 19th-century
paternalistic capitalist,
Paul Pfund, who
also built housing
and a music hall for
his workers.*

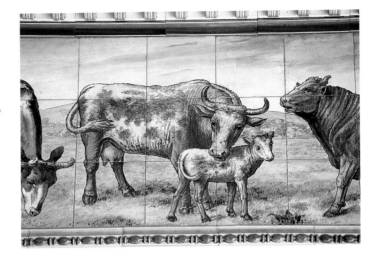

The shop survived the Second World
War because it was in the newer part of
the city that was not targeted by Allied
bombers. Then came the communists:
Pfund's was nationalized and neglected.
The tiles started to chip and crumble.

Shortly before the Iron Curtain
was lifted, a man called Wilfred Hensel
came across the border and captured
a moment in history by taking some
photographs of shops, including Pfund's.
He knew they were all about to change
drastically. 'The windows were empty,
and when you went inside, the shops
were empty too,' he said, adding that
in the dark days of communism people
used to join a queue without knowing
what it was for.

Wilfred Hensel and a partner went
on to buy Pfund's and spend years on
painstaking restorations. The shop now
gets 800,000 visitors a year – more, he
says, than all the other museums of
Dresden put together. It is not hard to
see the appeal: this is history you can
enjoy along with a plate of cheese and
a glass of the delicious local wine.

Above *The shop is completely covered in
hand-painted tiles that were lovingly restored
by experts after the fall of the Iron Curtain.*

Below *Pfund's favours unpasteurised French
cheeses, which are paired with wines from the
Elbe River valley. You can sample both in the
shop's café and restaurant.*

TAMBURINI

Delicatessen

FOUNDED *1932 by the brothers Angelo and Ferdinand Tamburini*

OWNERS *Ferdinand's son Giovanni and other family members*

SPECIALITIES *Food, in particular the specialities of Bologna: pasta, mortadella, salami, prosciutto*

ADDRESS/PHONE *Via Caprarie 1, 40124 Bologna, Italy; tel: (00 39) 051 234 726, fax: (00 39) 051 232 226*

E-MAIL/INTERNET *tambinfo@tin.it www.tamburini.com*

NEAR *City centre*

OPENING HOURS *Monday, Wednesday, Friday and Saturday 9am–7pm; Tuesday and Thursday 9am–2.30pm*

Bologna la grassa (Bologna the Fat) is the nickname of this most sensual of cities, and Tamburini's delicatessen celebrates the ways of the flesh with a gusto that makes you want to fling off your belt and grab the extra-virgin.

One counter is a white landscape of cheese, another a house built of meaty stones: coppa like fat-streaked marble, salamis as flecked as granite and smooth, pink rounds of mortadella, the latter so-named because the ingredients used to be pounded in a mortar. Hams and sausages fall from the ceiling in long curtains. Above the tables of the self-service restaurant hangs a carousel of hooks on which animals were butchered until 1975. Sixty pigs were killed every Monday and Thursday. The owner, Giovanni Tamburini, remembers the eager queues that formed to get the fresh livers.

There has been a meat market in this district since before Roman times. In the 1580s, the fleshy scenery of the area was depicted in an early painting by the artist Carachi, whose family included Bolognese butchers. (The original now resides in the picture gallery of Christ Church College, Oxford.)

Spread all around are the 300 dishes prepared daily, glistening with oil and a freshness that jumps out at your senses: the endives are chargrilled and lie overlapping on a platter like feathers on a wing; little onions marinate in vinegar; chicken salad is flecked with the deep purple of radicchio; the plump, succulent langoustines are dressed with lemon juice and rocket; meats roast on the wood-fired rôtisserie.

Giovanni is embarking on a journey to bring together the treasures of food from around Italy, an edible zoo that must be saved from the ever-present threat of European regulations. Let us hope that the delights on offer at Tamburini's register on the influential tastebuds of the politicians who drop by to visit Romano Prodi, the president of the European Commission and Giovanni's former professor, who has an office above the shop.

Recently, Giovanni re-formed the pop band of his youth. Their name? 'The Sensualists'.

Left *The centre of Bologna is a food-lover's paradise, with shop after shop stacked high with tempting food. After Tamburini's, visit the cake shop just down the road.*

Below *Giovanni Tamburini has made it his 'small mission' to promote artisan-crafted delicacies from all over Italy, including meats like these.*

ROSENDALS TRADGARD

Fruit & vegetables

FOUNDED *1985 by Lars Krantz and Tål Borg*
OWNER *Rosendals Trädgard Foundation*
SPECIALITIES *Biodynamic fruits, vegetables and flowers; home-grown and home-made food*
ADDRESS/PHONE *Rosendalsterrassen 12, 11521 Stockholm, Sweden; tel: (00 46) 8 545 812 70, fax: (00 46) 8 545 812 79*
INTERNET *www.rosendalstradgard.com*
LOCATED *On Djurgården island, last stop for Bus 47*
OPENING HOURS *7 March to 30 April: Tuesday to Sunday 10am–4pm; 1 May to 30 September: Tuesday to Sunday 10am–6pm; 1 October to 31 October: Tuesday to Sunday 10am–4pm; open in December for Christmas fair*

The people who come to Rosendals Trädgard are as important as the flowers, says Lars Krantz, co-founder of this garden of delights. 'There are children running on the grass, young people hugging under trees and old people eating cakes. It is like their home and their garden.'

The garden is on the royal island, the first of the 24,000 islands that make up the Stockholm archipelago, and has a holiday feel of drifting free from everyday life. There was a horticultural school here in the 19th century, and it has also been a royal park. Rosendals has opened up the space as a free place for people to spend time and shop. The gardeners here are happy to answer

Right *Rosendals pickles fruits and vegetables to preserve the summer produce. Rhubarb wine, mint and lemon cordial, dill oil, honey mustard, marinated goats cheeses, blood-orange jam and pickled cucumbers are just some of the foods on sale.*

Left *A place to be as much as a place to shop, Rosendals is a weekend garden retreat from city life.*

questions, there are courses on gardening and cooking, and people volunteer to work here, to be outside and to learn.

Rosendals adheres to biodynamic principles that follow the patterns of the moon. Just as the tides change with the moon, so the water in the soil and plants alter, and Rosendals believes that planting and cropping at the right time improves the plants' health and taste. No chemicals are needed.

The food shop is a paradise of beautiful, natural foods: jars of jam like big boiled sweets, chalky slabs of marinated goat's cheese, tiny yellow cherry tomatoes, earthy carrots, wonky peppers and bucketfuls of dill flowers. Delicious smells steal from the kitchen, tempting the senses with scents of cinnamon and bread fresh from the wood-fired oven.

Outside, people eat fresh, home-made food from the café. Beyond lie greenhouses, orchards, hen runs, long strips of cut-your-own flowers and banks of blossoms that quiver with bees.

JACOB HOOY

Herbs & spices

FOUNDED *1743 by Jacob Hooy, trading in the market; 1750 in the shop*

OWNERS: *Peter and Casper Oldenboom*

SPECIALITIES *Herbs and spices; special herbal mixtures for health and cooking*

ADDRESS/PHONE *Kloveniersburgwal 12, 1012 CT Amsterdam, Netherlands; tel: (00 31) 20 624 3041*

NEAR *Neuwmarkt; the red-light district*

OPENING HOURS *Monday and Wednesday to Friday 10am–6pm; Tuesday 8.15am–6pm; Saturday 8.15am–5pm*

Jacob Hooy is one of the oldest shops in Amsterdam, with a beauty that is aslant with age. The doorstep has been scooped smooth by 250 years of customers; the outside world is rippled by the ancient glass in the windows; and the shop's interior, lined with drawers and barrels labelled in old script, is a time warp.

The Oldenboom brothers have a worn metal card index with eight-generations' worth of herbal mixtures catalogued under headings such as 'Liver', 'Hayfever', 'Kidneys' and 'Relaxing Mixtures'. Herbal remedies such as these are coming back into fashion. More and more people visit the shop for St John's Wort, for example: a botanical stress reliever that has earned the nickname of 'nature's Prozac' in recent years. Specialists at the city's Lucas Hospital now send menopausal women to Jacob Hooy for a mixture that includes hops and valerian.

Near the shop entrance is a huge Indonesian carving made from a single piece of wood depicting a snake, the traditional sign of medicine. Underneath are jars containing 19 different kinds of liquorice, from the sweet to the salty.

Jacob Hooy stocks 400 different herbs and spices, meant for both health and cooking; there are mixtures for soups, fish and butter as well as those for aches and maladies. One customer comes all the way from Switzerland twice a year. When I visited, a no-nonsense Amsterdam matron was followed in by a New Age explorer in bunches, striped stockings and shades.

Left *Doctors send patients to this 18th-century pharmacy for herbal remedies, while cooks come in for herbs and spices. This particular customer wanted some saffron for a fish dish.*

Right *Herbs, spices, lotions and potions are contained in drawers and barrels labelled in old script.*

Below *Remedies, mixtures and arcane knowledge have been passed down through eight generations of the family. This battered box, hidden behind the counter, contains many tried-and-trusted shop secrets.*

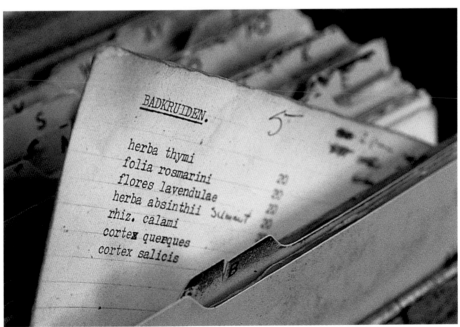

GEGENBAUER

Vinegars & pickled vegetables

FOUNDED *1929 by Ignaz Gegenbauer*

OWNER *Ignaz's grandson, Erwin Gegenbauer*

SPECIALITIES *Fruit vinegars, specialist wine vinegars, balsamic vinegars, high-quality pickled vegetables*

ADDRESS/PHONE *Stand 111–114 on the Naschmarkt; contact address: Waldgasse 3, A-1100 Vienna, Austria; tel: (00 43) 1 6041 0880, fax: (00 43) 1 6041 08822*

LOCATION *In the Naschmarkt, near Karlsplatz metro*

OPENING HOURS *Monday to Friday 9am–7pm; Saturday 8am–5pm*

Above *Gegenbauer is in the Naschmarkt: the street of stalls that is the culinary artery of Vienna.*

When Erwin Gegenbauer tells the wonderful story of his family's firm you can see how each generation has brought a fresh interpretation to the business, and that this is how it has survived and thrived.

When he began trading in 1929, Ignaz Gegenbauer specialized in sauerkraut and pickles, then a major source of vitamin C for the poor in Europe during winter. His son began to produce vinegar for the pickles, partly because his wife came from a wine-producing area. By 1994, when Erwin took over, the business had spread and the family had factories in Germany and Czechoslovakia. They sold a mass-produced commodity and were involved in the usual price-war tussles with supermarkets that beset many food producers, large and small.

Erwin is a food lover and a whisky connoisseur, who truffles out the best restaurants when he is travelling and who notices and relishes flavours. As a hobby, he had started to make his own vinegars from leftover wine. There was a 'eureka moment' when he found that different wines produced very different vinegars. This started off a line of experimentation on how to concentrate a particular flavour in a vinegar. Erwin began to make not just vinegars from particular wines but also fruit-wine vinegars from home-made fruit wines. These had far more flavour than the fruit vinegars made by the common method of steeping fruits in wine vinegar.

For all this work and inspiration, however, Erwin was still in charge of a business that marketed an industrial, mass-produced product. He decided upon radical change. The satellite factories were sold, and Gegenbauer's employees went down in number from 600 to 30. In future, the business would concentrate entirely on the careful production of craft vinegars.

The next step in the transformation was a very old-fashioned and effective form of marketing – literally, marketing – the new products. The Naschmarkt lies in the gutsy heart of Vienna. It is the culinary artery through which pumps a mix of races, the rich, the poor, actors, politicians, intellectuals, amateur cooks, journalists, and chefs. Erwin's grandfather dragged his cart by foot to the Naschmarkt until he got a horse in the 1940s. His grandmother kept her baby warm wrapped in newspaper there. Erwin's father, an energetically creative man, always said the best place to market-research a new product was here; in the Naschmarkt, customers spoke their minds and if they went for something, it would sell anywhere.

When Erwin stepped out, for the first time, at the family stall, his knees were shaking. A customer came up and asked if he knew anything about vinegar and then proceeded to display a wide knowledge of the subject himself.

The whole day was an unforgettable experience and Erwin still likes to spend Saturdays on the stall, in direct contact with the customers. When the business

Below *Vegetables and fruits are pickled in their own vinegars; here, for example, peppers are preserved in a special pepper vinegar, and pickled cucumbers are sold in cucumber vinegar.*

began to change, he told his plans to
the two women who had worked on
the stall for 40 years. A week later
they came back and said, yes, it's good.
They were crucial, he says, because the
bridge between customer and producer
must have no holes.

Meanwhile, Erwin continues to
experiment. The wines for the specialized
wine vinegars come from top producers,
who also understand what he is doing
better than lesser vineyard owners who
object to their wine being turned into
vinegar. Erwin recently perfected a
delicious Pedro Ximénez sherry vinegar,
and he continues to produce new fruit
vinegars with distinct flavours, such as
quince, melon, tomato, and single-apple
varieties, like James Grieve and Golden
Delicious. Then there are the balsamic
vinegars made by cooking, reducing and

Above *Wine vinegars and specialised
fruit vinegars are the foundation of
Gegenbauer's new business. The sellers
use pipettes to give customers samples
of each product.*

Right *A bottle of single-variety Golden
Delicious apple vinegar. Gegenbauer tries
to capture the essence of a single flavour
in each vinegar.*

maturing such wines as elderberry, plum
and peach. In a further development,
Gegenbauer now pickles fruits and
vegetables in vinegars of their own
flavours: cucumbers in cucumber vinegar,
red cabbage and quince in red cabbage
vinegar, dried figs in fig vinegar, dried
apricots in apricot vinegar. Once again,
Erwin is dealing with the supermarkets,
but this time on his own terms.

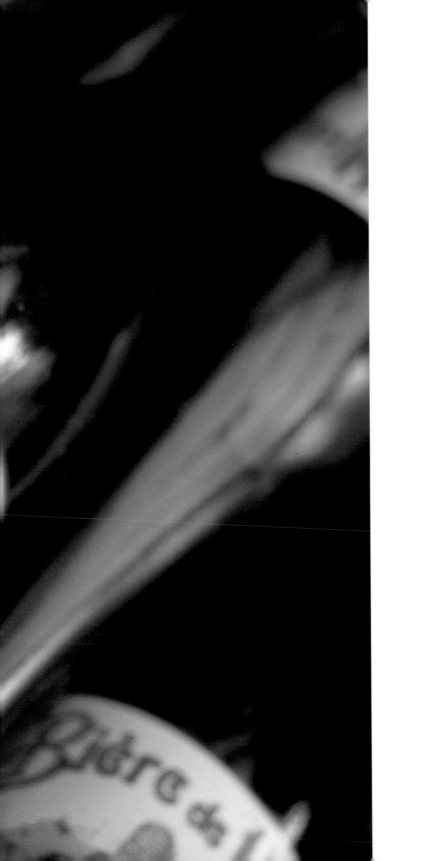

THE CUP THAT CHEERS

SIBYLLANS COFFEE AND TEA SHOP

Coffee & tea

FOUNDED *1916 by Hilmer Hansson*
OWNER *Hilmer's grandson, Jörgen Hansson*
SPECIALITIES *Coffee and tea*
ADDRESS/PHONE *Sibyllegatan 35, Stockholm, Sweden; tel: (00 46) 8 662 0663*
NEAR *On Ostermalm island, bus routes 62 (also 55 and 41)*
OPENING HOURS *Monday to Friday 9.30am–6pm*

On roasting days at Sibyllans, it's easy to tell which way the wind is blowing by watching the direction from which the customers come. Coffee is roasted in a low-ceilinged room piled high with sacks of beans, mostly imported from producers the Hanssons have got to know personally over the years. Another room is so stuffed with bags that the owner's son practises his drums in the sound-proofed space.

It is no surprise that Sweden is home to this gem of a shop. The Scandinavian countries are the biggest consumers of coffee in the world, and Sweden has a per capita consumption almost double that of Italy. Coffee wards off the cold of the long, hard winters – sometimes with a little help. Frank Hansson, of the second generation of shopowners, tells a tipsy tale of how people used to put a small coin in a cup of coffee, then add aquavit until the coin could be seen again.

It was Frank's father, Hilmer, who started the shop when he did a good deal on a small amount of coffee and it disappeared 'like butter in the sun'. The only dip in quality came with the war years, when the Hanssons had to roast barley and rye as coffee substitutes.

Nowadays, people are turning to the dark, Continental blends and drinking more tea, the other speciality of the shop. The Swedes are tea connoisseurs and many prefer loose leaves to bags.

Once, a Swedish journalist went to London in search of the best cup of tea in Europe and interviewed the head of Twinings – who told him to go back to his own country and Sibyllans.

Hilmer's brother came up with a special secret blend called Sir William's, which is one of the shop's best-sellers. It is delicious with a slice of orange.

Left *Customers are offered samples of tea to smell as an aid in making their choices. Some of the teas are blended in an orange cement mixer in one of the shop's back rooms.*

Right *These chrome containers from the Twenties, the gold stars on the glass ceiling and 160 kinds of tea and coffee make Sibyllans one of the most splendid shops in Stockholm.*

BERRY BROS & RUDD

Wines

FOUNDED *1699*

OWNERS *Now into the eighth generation of family members*

SPECIALITIES *Wines and spirits, particularly claret, German wines, vintage port and Cutty Sark whisky*

ADDRESS/PHONE *3 St James's Street, London SW1A 1EG; tel: 020 7396 9669, fax: 01256 340106*

INTERNET *www.bbr.co.uk*

MAIL ORDER *Free delivery to the UK mainland for orders over £100; flat rate carriage fee of £7.50 for orders under £100*

NEAR *Piccadilly and Green Park Underground stations*

OPENING HOURS *Monday to Friday 9am–5.30pm; Saturday 10am–4pm*

Berry Bros has no counter and very few bottles on view. Instead, you sit down and peruse a list until one of the assistants is free to help and to fetch your purchases from the cellars. There is plenty to look at while you wait: the place is a living museum. Every so often they discover something at the back of a drawer that has been there for decades, and sometimes it ends up in this room on discreet display.

Until a few years ago, shutters across the inside of the windows shrouded the front room in a Cruikshank-like gloom. One day, the window cleaner was late and the shutters were left open. The shop's owners 'saw the light' and left them them that way, although there was some shock at the change ('Good heavens! People might look *in*!').

London's St James's has an old-fashioned, masculine atmosphere; it's a place where a gentleman might sort his shoes, gun and cigars before going in to his club. Berry Bros retains that august whiff of location and history. However, new technology has enabled the business to continue and develop its commitment to old-fashioned personal service.

A computer brings an account customer's details on screen even as an employee picks up the phone call. (This being Berry Bros, the computer screens in the shop have wooden frames and fit seamlessly into the 17th-century interior.) Today, some 60,000 customers can be sent a mail-shot with ease; whereas in the 1920s, staff stayed on for an extra hour for two or three weeks to

Left *Berry Bros' splendid sign is actually a coffee mill – an allusion to the shop's origins, when it sold groceries as well as wines and spirits.*

Right *Some of the antique bottles kept in a case at the back of the Berry Bros shop.*

address envelopes for a mail-shot about the greatest vintage of the century, the 1921 Hock and Mosel.

Customers in the shop (and you can go in for a single bottle of house wine at under £4) are surrounded by centuries of history. On the right as you enter, lurching tipsily on an old floor that slopes like the deck of a ship at sea, is a display of teeny bottles that were spares

Above *The front room of Berry Bros, where customers wait for their wines to be brought up from the cellars. It is full of old objects to examine.*

Left *Wines being transferred from the cellars – still in the old-fashioned way.*

Right *Berry Bros historic cellars below the shop. Part of these have been converted into an atmospheric space for tastings and parties.*

from the wine cellar made by Francis Berry for Queen Mary's dolls' house. He reduced real labels photographically for the purpose, and even filled all 66 dozen bottles with genuine vintage wines and spirits – first letting the Champagne go flat, however, because the bubbles would have been too big for the bottles' tiny necks.

At the back of the shop are some real-sized antique bottles that would have been far more valuable in their time for their glass rather than their contents. Each bottle bears the name of its owner on the outside; the wines were kept in casks and decanted.

Then there are the famous scales that have weighed such esteemed customers as Lord Byron and Lord Laurence Olivier: their ups and downs recorded in a set of red leather books, with a separate volume for 'Ladies'. Here and there excuses have been noted in the margins: 'frock coat' or even 'muddy boots' (the Aga Khan, December 16, 1932). On a wall nearby is a framed letter from the owners of the Titanic informing Berry Bros about an unfortunate incident with an iceberg.

When Berry Bros first opened its doors for trading, St James's was one of the most powerful streets in the world, down which passed the rich and influential. Now the wines reach such customers by other means: Berry Bros sells on the Internet, and has established a branch at Heathrow Airport.

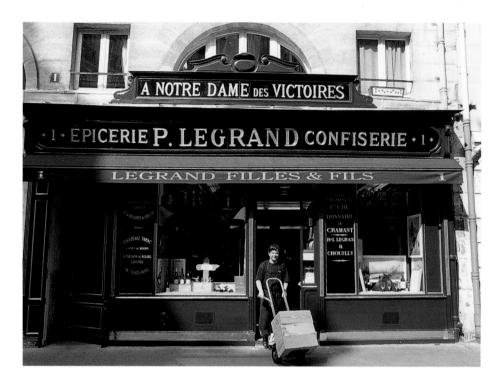

LEGRAND FILLES & FILS

Wines

FOUNDED *1880 by M Beaugé*

OWNER *Members of the Legrand family since 1919; current director Francine Legrand*

SPECIALITIES *Wines, spirits and their paraphernalia; chocolates, sweets, groceries*

ADDRESS/PHONE *1 rue de la Banque, 75002 Paris, France; tel: (00 33) 1 42 60 07 12, fax: (00 33) 1 42 61 25 51*

NEAR *Bourse métro*

MAIL ORDER *Available, plus the cost of postage and packing. Wines are also stocked in London and are available by mail order from Villandry: 170 Great Portland Street, London; tel: 020 7631 3131*

OPENING HOURS: *Tuesday to Friday 9am–7.30pm; Saturday 8.30am–1pm and 3pm–7pm*

Twin brothers married two sisters and then went off to war for seven years. The women ran an *épicerie-confiserie* and when the men returned they all moved into this larger shop so that there would be room enough for everyone.

It was Lucien Legrand, the next generation, who expanded the business's wine selection. A sense of his character can be gained by looking at the ceiling. At first glance, it appears to be covered in a textured, patterned fabric. In fact, it is made of hundreds and hundreds of corks stuck there by Lucien in the sweltering summer of 1976.

Of his nine children, three sons and two daughters tried and failed to work with the patriarch. It was Francine –

Right *A Parisian wine shop with a feminine twist, Legrand was set up by two women whose husbands had gone off to war.*

chic, petite, charming as a songbird – who survived. Perhaps she has inherited some of her father's will.

Francine regulary tours the country, going off the beaten track to search out special wines. She looks for those that are well made and then have something extra. Outstanding winemakers, she says, have two characteristics: they are at once active and contemplative – the craftsman and the artist.

The interior of the shop may be old, but the atmosphere is light-hearted and modern. Legrand still stocks chocolates, tins of fish, even foie gras in a chilled brass-and-wood cabinet, and it is this range – the touch of carnival – that attracts a varied clientele. Some come in for a *grand cru*, others for biscuits and a fresh wine to end the day. It is a feminine sort of wine shop: as Francine says, with a teasing rise to her lips, some men are proud of their knowledge of labels, but some women are less prejudiced about appreciating the contents of the bottles.

Left *Little satiny sweets, Brittany sea-salt, spices, olive oil, biscuits, pâtés and chocolates sit alongside wines that have been sought out from all over France.*

BEER MANIA

Belgian beer

FOUNDED *1983 by Nasser Eftekhari*

OWNER *Nasser Eftekhari*

SPECIALITIES *400 Belgian beers, beer glasses, beer hampers*

ADDRESS/PHONE *Chaussée de Wavre 174–176, 1050 Brussels, Belgium; tel: (00 32) 2 512 1788; fax: (00 32) 2 511 32 42*

EMAIL/INTERNET *beermania@skynet.be www.beermania.com*

NEAR *Porte de Namur métro*

MAIL ORDER *The price list may be found on the website; postage and packing costs £19 for 48 bottles to the UK mainland (not N Ireland)*

OPENING HOURS *Monday to Saturday (and Sundays in December) 11am–7pm*

Before he opens up at 11am, Nasser Eftekhari has been tasting, buying and collecting beers from the breweries that dot the Belgian countryside. These traditional breweries used to produce mostly for the local community, making special beers for Christmas, the seasons and the annual fair. Yet while other traditional crafts have faded and all but died, Belgian beers have gone from strength to strength, achieving international fame.

When Nasser came to Belgium, some would say it was by accident; he says it was fate. Born in Iran where he enjoyed beer from the age of 13, he was forced by the fundamentalist revolution to make his own beer in secret at home, risking imprisonment, adding yeast and sugar to alcohol-free brews. In his early twenties,

he escaped and came (by accident or fate) to the connoisseur's beer country.

Nasser opened a shop and amassed a selection of around 400 beers, from the obscure to the famous. Others may have made more money – one man asked a thousand questions and went on to become a millionaire as the largest importer of Belgian beer to the United States – but Nasser's approach is rich in many ways. He loves the way the small breweries have survived and thrived; he loves the depth of knowledge of the brewers; he loves the beers. Beer is a democratic drink, he says, because the best is not so very expensive.

Some bottles have been maturing since Nasser bought them in the early days; not for sale, however – they are for friends or special occasions. Behind his desk lurks a ten-year-old bottle of Duval to toast the birth of his child.

SWEET TREATS

ESCRIBA

Cakes & chocolate

FOUNDED 1906 by Mateu Serra and Josefa Gala Roses

OWNER Members of the Escriba family, now in the fourth generation

SPECIALITIES Cakes and chocolates; cake creations for Barcelona's Easter parade

ADDRESS/PHONE Rambla de les Flors 83, Barcelona, Spain; tel: (00 34) 93 301 60 27. The original shop is at Gran Via 546; tel: (00 34) 93 454 75 35, fax: (00 34) 93 454 69 12

NEAR Metro Liceu

OPENING HOURS Every day, including Sunday, 8am–9pm

The pages of the photograph album flick by as Antoni Escriba proudly displays his life in cakes and chocolate. First comes a confectionery sculpture he swapped with Miró for a Picasso engraving. (Antoni says he added some watercolours as an 'improvement'. Really? I ask several times. Yes, he says, his smile becoming more and more mischievous.) Then there is a topless Cleopatra jumping out of a sweet pyramid; a transvestite in a high meringue periwig wandering through a banquet saying 'eat me, lick me'; a woman in a sandwich.

Next he displays a cake exploding with sparks, followed by a drifting fall of rose petals; a note from the Pope; a photo of an award ceremony with white, torque-topped chefs filling the concentric circles of the European Parliament building, and Antoni on the stage with his family. There is also a photo of Antoni dressed like a Roman general at the reins of a team of plumed white horses, leading in a cake to feed 12,000 guests.

The pictures that makes him pause the longest, however, do not contain a single sweet crumb or a gleam of sugar. One is Antoni passing on the Olympic flame at the opening of the 1992 games in Barcelona; a local celebrity, he was part of the team for this intimidating task. The other picture is on a brochure. It shows Antoni with his young grandson stirring a bowl of melted chocolate, the young, unmarked face looking up at the old man, who has a bit of chocolate on his index finger.

He talks again and again of the importance of passing the business on to his sons and knowing the right time to go. As he speaks, the baker/confectioner links his fingers to illustrate the strength, flexibility and durability of a chain.

Left *Escriba is situated in a former pasta shop; it boasts one of the best* modernisme *exteriors in Barcelona, dating from 1902. The front room has beautiful old wooden drawers and the back room is lined with photographs of celebrities, such as Spanish film director Pedro Almódovar, and their customized cakes.*

Right *Escriba's cakes and chocolates have a bold, modern look. They are sold to customers to take away in smart boxes or to be eaten at the back of the shop.*

IL GELATO DI SAN CRISPINO

Ice-cream

FOUNDED *1993 by Giuseppe, Pasquale and Paola Alongi*

OWNERS *Giuseppe and Pasquale Alongi and the Nesci family*

SPECIALITIES *Ice-cream and sorbet (zabaione is a particularly famous flavour)*

ADDRESS/PHONE *Via Panetteria 42, Rome, Italy; tel: (00 39) 06 679 3924. The original shop is at via Acaia 56–56a, San Giovanni*

NEAR *The Trevi fountain; Barberini metro*

OPENING HOURS *Monday and Wednesday to Sunday 12 noon–12.30am; closed Tuesday*

The Alongis do not advertise, but several guidebooks acclaim their ice-cream as the best in Italy, so there is no need. San Crispino is less flamboyant than other *gelateria*: there are no crested waves of splashy Versace colours, no scattered fruits. And no cones – absolutely not. These contain artificial additives that are anathema to San Crispino's philosophy. So, it's tubs only.

The business was set up by two brothers, Giuseppe and Pasquale Alongi, and Giuseppe's wife, Paola. They started to make ice-cream at home and soon realized that what they produced was in a different league to what was available commercially. The secret lies in the freshness and quality of ingredients. The sweet shock of the lemon sorbet comes from Amalfi lemons; the coffee from Blue Mountain beans; the deeply, richly boozy *zabaione* is flavoured with a 20-year-old Marsala.

Fruits are only sold in season, with the late-summer redcurrants, raspberries and peaches giving way in early autumn to pear, pomegranate and a fragrant grape sorbet made from the *uva fragola* variety, which has a hint of strawberries. Anything unsold at the end of the day is thrown away: at San Crispino they start afresh each morning.

These ices slip into your mouth like melting silk and achieve the essence of flavour. The hazelnut has a rich toastiness, the blackberry a mellow perfume, the raspberry a sharp sweetness that lingers on your taste buds for long, delicious seconds; the chocolate is dark velvet. The meringue with toasted hazelnuts and meringue with chocolate both capture the fragile explosions of sugar and stickiness of a meringue.

It has been said that a day in Italy without ice-cream is a day wasted. How true. This being the case, you should work your way through every single flavour here – then try them all again in judiciously planned combinations.

Left *Customers come until midnight to buy ice-creams to eat while strolling the streets of Rome.*

Right *The ice-cream at San Crispino is kept in deep, metal containers to keep it cold. It contains no preservatives or stabilizers to prevent it from melting at higher temperatures.*

LA MAISON DU MIEL

Honey

FOUNDED *1898 by Charles Galland*
OWNER *Members of the Galland family*
SPECIALITIES *Honeys from all over France*
ADDRESS/PHONE *24 rue Vignon, 75009 Paris,
France; tel/fax: (00 33) 1 47 42 26 70*
NEAR *Place de la Madeleine; Madeleine métro*
MAIL ORDER *Products available in London
and by mail order at Villandry: 170 Great
Portland Street; tel: 020 7631 3131 (see also
Legrand Filles & Fils, pages 46–47)*
OPENING HOURS *Monday to Saturday
9.15am–7pm*

Below *La Maison du Miel (the House
of Honey) has customers who have been
regulars for more than 60 years and who,
like the shop's owners, firmly believe that
honey is a health food.*

It was closed during the Second World
War and used as a hideaway for the
Resistance, otherwise La Maison du Miel
has stayed open for three generations.

At the front of the counter are some
35 pots for tasting: everything from light,
floral types to the antiseptic, almost
savoury tang of buckwheat honey from the
Canadian prairies. At the back are four
large drums of honey on tap; they change
according to what's best at the time.

La Maison is unusual not just for this
wide range of flavours but for what goes
on behind the scenes. The letters 'UA'
on the logo stand for *Union Abriculteurs*
(Union of Honey-makers), because the
shop was set up to bring honeys from
all over France to the capital. A wide
network of apiarists has been established,

Above *Many of the honeys have their health-giving properties listed in English on a leaflet. Orange-blossom honey is good for insomnia and calming children; thyme honey stimulates the digestion; rosemary is good for asthma and the liver; fir is a general antiseptic.*

Below *Four drums dispense a changing range of flavours such as lavender, Alpine, thyme, rhododendron and lime blossom. Unusual kinds of honey on sale include a mint honey from Oregon and a bitter-holly honey from Maine.*

and every year they offer the shop the best of their produce, sending in samples that are tasted and tested before the final selection is made. On top of this, the Gallands themselves have 700 hives that are driven by night around the countryside to farmers who pay for the bees to come and pollinate their plants.

La Maison du Miel treats honey in a very French manner: with a degree of seriousness. Leaflets list the health properties of the golden-brown potion, and none of the honey is pasteurised because this would destroy the goodness and flavour. The recommended 'dose' is five teaspoons a day – sweet medicine! It is no surprise that La Maison has regular customers who have themselves spanned the 20th century.

WITTAMER

Cakes

FOUNDED *1910 by Henri Wittamer*
OWNER *Members of the Wittamer family*
SPECIALITIES *Pâtisserie and chocolates*
ADDRESS/PHONE *6-12-13 Place du Grand Sablon, B-1000 Brussels, Belgium; tel: (00 31 2) 512 37 42, fax: (00 32 2) 512 52 09*
E-MAIL *wittamer@megasite.be*
NEAR *Porte de Namur métro; Au Grand Rasoir knife shop (see pages 86–87)*
MAIL ORDER *DHL service for chocolates*
OPENING HOURS *Monday 10am–6pm; Tuesday to Sunday 7am–7pm*

Below *The café tables on Brussels's Place du Grand Sablon: a smart address full of chic shops.*

The cakes in the window are as chic as Paris hats, every form and flourish a delight. Tarts swell with fruit just too poised to tumble; chocolate icing gleams, as dark and glossy as black glass; paper-thin slices of pear fan out like a hand of cards. Many cakes are light as Paris hats, too, which is a surprise.

Wittamer was opened by the hard-working Henri Wittamer. Orphaned at the age of nine, he worked on farms and then served an apprenticeship at a *boulangerie* before starting his own business. His son transformed the shop from a neighbourhood bakery into a renowned *pâtisserie*; at the same time, the Place Sablon became as smart as the cakes. Affluent citizens now aspire to gain some of their padding at Wittamer's

café tables, and chefs and apprentice chefs come from all over the world to work and learn in the kitchens; at one count, the number of different nationalities 'in residence' was 18.

At present, the business is run by the third generation of Wittamers, Paul and Myriam. Born and brought up above the shop, Myriam remembers sneaking downstairs to raid the fridges when her schoolfriends stayed the night. Now she oversees the shop and business with an eagle eye for detail.

Down the road is the Wittamer chocolate shop. It delivers by courier all over the world but, if you wish to shop like the Sultan of Brunei, you are free to send a private plane to collect your 100kg for Christmas.

DE TAART VAN M'N TANTE

Modern cakes

FOUNDED 1990 by Siemon de Jong

OWNER Siemon de Jong and Noam Offer

SPECIALITIES Contemporary cakes made
to order

ADDRESS/PHONE Eerste Jacob van
Campenstraat 35, 1072 BC Amsterdam,
Netherlands; tel: (00 31) 20 776 4600,
fax: (00 31) 20 776 4604

E-MAIL info@detaartvanmijntante.a2000.nl

NEAR Rijksmuseum; Van Gogh Museum;
T'Mannetje bicycle shop (see pages 82–83)

OPENING HOURS Monday to Saturday
9am–5pm, by appointment

'Porno and cakes are a great combination,
so long as it tastes good,' says Siemon de
Jong, a confectioner with a contemporary
slant on sweet delight. His sponges and
ganaches are all in the best possible taste;
the designs based on optical illusions,
architecture – or toilets.

The shop is a homely kitchen where
you are offered a glass of lemonade
and a slice of cake. Siemon's parents
have retired, but they still help out
with the business, and his father grows
apples for the Dutch apple cakes.
At the front is a computer that runs a
slide show all night. It caught my eye as
I passed by one evening and wondered
what on earth a cake was doing with
no clothes on.

Left *A batch of fruitcakes being prepared. When they are ready, they will become the base of some of today's spectacular creations.*

Right *The designs for a gay couple's wedding cake. People come in with their wildest fantasies which Siemon tries to turn into edible reality. The cakes must be able to stand up and survive the party, before they are cut up and devoured.*

Below *The final cake, complete with a gay wedding couple on top. Co-owner Noam Offer had recently been to Britain hunting for wedding figures for the cakes.*

Siemon's passion for baking started when he was working as a nurse in New York and living with his boyfriend: 'I was in love, so I made him cakes,' he explains. He returned to Amsterdam and set up on his own business after learning in other kitchens, arriving at his current situation, as the saying goes, 'by 13 trades and 12 accidents'.

The shop is alive with the impulse of delight that lies behind the art of confectionery. Simeon loves word-play and visual puns, and this playfulness shows in his work. For a food fashion show, he dressed a model in a Mary Quant dress of linked Stroopwafel biscuits and another in a Golden Age suit made of dyed pancakes arranged like pieces of suede and topped by a doily ruff.

Wedding couples are sometimes anxious about touching this type of edible art, but Siemon's response is that cutting a cake is a ritual slaughter: it should be treated as an offering to the event.

LolaKopf   F8557

HOBBIES AND HARDWARE

37

2.80

ROBERT CRESSER

Brushes & brooms

FOUNDED *1873 by Robert Cresser*
OWNER *Stephen Gilhooly and Gary Turner*
SPECIALITIES *Natural fibre brushes designed*
for serious scrubbing
ADDRESS/PHONE *40 Victoria Street, Edinburgh*
EH1 2JW; tel/fax: 0131 225 2181
NEAR *The Grassmarket; the Royal Mile*
MAIL ORDER *Available, plus the cost of p&p*
OPENING HOURS *Monday to Saturday*
9am–5pm

Right *Cresser's stocks natural fibre brushes*
of every shape, size and speciality.

Every brush in Robert Cresser's has its business – sometimes two. The ridged library model reaches the tops of books on shelves; the spokey, once used for the wheels of vintage cars, fits neatly into that awkward space between radiator and wall; teapot-spout brushes are sold in sets of four or six to clean bagpipes.

There used to be three brush shops in this area. Cresser's has survived partly through hard work: staff still go knocking on doors every day for sales and repairs. It is graft in general that keeps the place alive, for these brushes are the scrubbers of runways and pubs, railway platforms and power stations.

The patrons are as varied as the brushes. One family comes back once a generation to have a set of silver-backed brushes repaired. Then there are tourists who cannot get over the glamour of a hardware shop where pairs and quartets of brushes line the front as if awaiting the music of *The Sorcerer's Apprentice*.

Some brushes are not for sale. Hidden behind the counter or hanging from the ceiling, they were donated by customers. One such is a tailor's brush that was used to brush upwards (never downwards) to avoid putting a sheen on cloth. It is so softly luxuriant that you want to stroke it like a cat.

DIE IMAGINARE MANUFAKTUR

Brushes & brooms

FOUNDED *In the1920s by the Berlin Institute for the Blind; relaunched in 1998*

OWNER *Berlin Institute for the Blind*

SPECIALITIES *Contemporary and traditional brushes, wickerwork and mats*

ADDRESS/PHONE *Oranienstrasse 26, D-01999 Berlin, Germany; tel: (00 49) 30 2588 6614, fax: (00 49) 30 2588 6615*

INTERNET *www.blindenanstalt.de*

NEAR *Kottbusser Tor U-Bahn 1, 12 and 15 in Kreuzberg*

MAIL ORDER *Products are stocked in London by Babylon, Fulham Road; tel: 020 7376 7355*

OPENING HOURS *Monday to Thursday 9am–4.45pm; Friday 9am–3.45pm*

The Berlin Institute for the Blind, in Kreuzberg, a part of Berlin that once bordered the Wall, had run a business that made and sold traditional brushes, matting and wickerwork for most of the century. Business, however, was falling dramatically. Fortunately, across the road, a design company noticed the situation and offered to help.

The idea was to combine traditional handiwork with modern design. First, the designers spent several months getting to

Below *Die Imaginäre Manufaktur (literally, the 'Atelier of the Mind's Eye') was a traditional shop that has been transformed by a modern design company.*

know the workshop so that change could be an evolution and not a ripping jolt. Then they came up with ideas on how to adapt brushes to a modern home.

A fine-dusting model was put on a stylish china base and turned into an ultra-soft body brush. Mats were layered, buckled and stitched to make an eco-trendy bottle rack. A circular brush was put on its end to make an alternative egg cup; bottle brushes were joined and bent over to make fruit bowls. Photo frames, flowerpots, key holders, pen holders: the place bristled with ideas and energy. Old broom heads, which were getting damp in a cellar, were piled up in the window marked with '1,000-750-500-250 brushes', like a church spire appeal. They sold like hotcakes.

In just nine months, business trebled. New life was injected into the tradition of a craft atelier. Today, workers take a quiet pride in knowing that their products are appreciated by customers as far afield as America, Japan and England.

Above *This front window display has sold 750 of a thousand brushes using a simple, old-fashioned technique: pile it high.*

Below *Modern design combines with old-fashioned craft for these soft body brushes.*

ROBERT MILLS,
ARCHITECTURAL ANTIQUES

Architectural salvage

FOUNDED *1980 by Robert Mills*

OWNER *Robert Mills*

SPECIALITIES *Architectural salvage, especially neo-Gothic church woodwork and Victorian pub interiors: all original, no reproductions*

ADDRESS/PHONE *Narroways Road, Eastville, Bristol BS2 9XB; tel: 0117 955 6542, fax: 0117 955 8146*

E-MAIL/INTERNET
robert.mills.ltd@dial.pipex.com
www.architecturalantiques.co.com

NEAR *Ikea in Eastville; the M32*

MAIL ORDER *A catalogue is produced regularly; personalized catalogues can be arranged*

OPENING HOURS *Monday to Friday 9.30am–5.30pm*

Where do old shops, churches and pubs go to when they die? If they are lucky, to the limbo of a reclamation yard. If not, for the axe and the flames. Bob Mills started trading in architectural salvage after he watched an Anglican church in Liverpool go up in smoke and the stained glass smashed for a few pounds of lead.

In this warehouse on the edge of Bristol, the stripped bones of buildings await resurrection. Flights of steps lead to nowhere; doors are stacked like packs of cards; piles of pews are on sale for £200 or so a throw; white and gold Italian confectioners' shelves, shorn of their sweets, sit patiently, one of the prettier orphans on offer. They won't be there for as long as the enormous circus awning, a vaudeville white elephant still looking for a home.

When Bob started, most of his clients were abroad. 'People in England feel guilty that they don't go to Sunday school; they get vibes around anything religious,' he explains. Buyers come in waves. Forty-foot truckloads used to go to Germany, where there is more of a tradition of domestic Gothic furniture. The Japanese developed a taste for white weddings in rooms fitted out like

churches, complete with hymn-singing choirs. A client invited Bob over to one such secular church named in his honour: 'St Robert'. The Japanese also had a phase of looking for entire buildings to be moved to Japan for golf clubhouses.

More recently, there has been an upsurge in British and Irish pubs and clubs being kitted out in bits of old buildings. Confession boxes make good telephone booths and showers. The home market has become less queasy about church furnishings and less snobbish about neo-gothic decorative art in general. A friend of Bob's has a neo-Gothic kitchen, where hi-tech hides behind high church, cookbooks open like

Left *A lectern and other bits and pieces of church furnishings and architecture.*

Below *Doors, pews, roofs and entire wooden rooms await buyers, who come to Robert Mills from all over the world.*

the Bible on a brass stand, and holiday snaps slide into the hymn board.

Taking out the inside of a building can modernize and reinvigorate its use: a church that once had rigid staves of pews becomes more practical with moveable, comfortable chairs. But if there is a slight note of regret for Bob, who is a keen Anglican, it is that modern church decoration is so often of a lower standard.

Nowadays, old properties are more valued and Bob is no longer offered the guts of two or three churches a week. Prices have risen – and fewer angels end up on the scrapheap.

Wandering around this building of buildings you get a slightly eerie sense of all the lives these doors and walls have surrounded. They are the surviving works of specialized craftsworkers of other ages. They were

Above *Part of an old merry-go-round that is looking for a new lease of life.*

Right *The treasure trove of English neo-Gothic inside the warehouse, on the outskirts of Bristol. Robert Mills currently has one customer who is in the process of kitting out an entire palace in Guatemala with shipments of stock – like a modern-day William Randolph Hearst.*

not entirely the 'good old days' of craftsmanship, however. Bob Mills' team knows from the removal of some Victorian churches that cowboy building practices are nothing new.

Occasionally, secrets are revealed. During the renovation of a French sideboard, a copy of Victor Hugo's radical paper *L'Evénement* was found. It had been stuffed inside the furniture by artisans who were laughing behind the backs of the bourgeois owners.

DEYROLLE

Taxidermy & natural history

FOUNDED *1831*
OWNERS *Nathalie and Anne Orlowska*
SPECIALITIES *Taxidermy, natural history and geology*
ADDRESS/PHONE *46 rue du Bac, 75007 Paris, France; tel: (00 33) 1 42 22 30 07, fax: (00 33) 1 42 22 32 02*
NEAR *Métro rue du Bac*
OPENING HOURS *Monday to Saturday 10am–6.45pm*

The stuffed animals are so naturalistic that the whole place is fascinating rather than mustily creepy. A cat naps, curled up in a pram. A lioness rests near her inquisitive cub. A zebra prances and a dog looks at you around a display case, alert and ready to bark at the intruder. Strange to say, Deyrolle is full of life, albeit caught in a three-dimensional freeze-frame.

People bring in their deceased pets with favourite photographs so that they can be posed just so, the right stretch of neck and the particular curl of tail giving them everlasting vitality. Each animal is stored in a deep-freeze until the taxidermists are ready to take off the skin to tan and remould it over sculpted stuffing.

Domestic pets are harder to skin because they are more fatty than wild animals. The protected species come from zoos and are popular in the growing market for rentals for parties and film sets. You may see a full-grown polar bear with its fur dyed pink being loaded into a van, or two men carrying a zebra downstairs on its way to a film launch. The business also does sporting trophies, a more old-fashioned source of income.

Deyrolle is housed in the home of Samuel Bernard, a banker of Louis XIV in the 17th century. It became a shop in 1831 and seems to have barely stepped out of the 19th century. You can spend hours and hours wandering over the creaky parquet looking at the animals and going through drawers stuffed with surprises, such as a bunch of eyes on wires, which stare up at you like surrealist flowers. The back room is a stilled universe of insects, the flutter and patterned colours of butterflies and moths pinned down forever.

All over the shop are unusual items: coat racks made of bent hooves; old natural history posters (the dissection of a nose, the origins of chocolate, earthworms, flowers and various whats, hows and whys); a small frame containing 300 or so tiny phosphorescent beetles from the Midi, squared up like modern art of the pointillist school.

Small children pat the animals, dogs bark at them. Older children unleash their curiosity, excited by standing next to a polar bear without bars. Some of the older customers have asked if they themselves can be stuffed. Deyrolle declines. But when you think about it, can there be a higher compliment for the taxidermist's art?

Left *A llama looks down at the passing Parisian traffic on the Rive Gauche.*

Right *Staff carrying off a zebra for hire. Deyrolle stuffs everything from small sporting trophies to large animals from zoos. The taxidermists study nature to make the animals as life-like as possible.*

HOLZAPFEL

Tools

FOUNDED 1997 by Alexis Zweifler

OWNER Alexis Zweifler

SPECIALITIES Tools and blades from around the world, Japanese saws, Japanese tools made by master blacksmiths

ADDRESS/PHONE Kollwitzstrasse 100, 10435 Berlin, Germany; tel: (00 49) 304 40520 04, fax: (00 49) 30 789 90611

E-MAIL holzapfel@knuut.de

NEAR Eberswalder U-Bahn 2; Prenzlauer Allee S-Bahn 8

MAIL ORDER A brochure is available (in German)

OPENING HOURS Monday to Friday 11.30am–6.30pm; Saturday 11.30am–2.30pm

Above Alexis Zweifler using one of the super-light Japanese saws. Note the work-bench at the side for customers to try out the tools.

Some people who come into Holzapfel do not have a clue about carpentry; they just want to look at the tools because they are so artfully arranged. Then there are the brickies and chippies, in Berlin from all over Europe to rebuild and restore the city as a capital. They come in for sexy American hammers and other top kit.

The shop was set up by a carpenter when he could not get good tools and was tired of grumpy shopkeepers. In the window is a postcard with a joke that roughly translates as, 'There are three rules for running a shop – and we don't know them.' Alexis Zweifler does. In no particular order they are: friendliness, the ability and will to explain, and, of course, quality.

Alexis has searched the world for the best blades and found many of them in Japan, where the Samurai fostered a tradition of expert blacksmiths. The first time he used one of the light, flexible Japanese saws, it turned wood to butter. It took a year of ping-ponged faxes and visits to establish a trading link with these dedicated masters: respect takes time. Some tools also need to be earned, such as a plane made by a 70-year-old master craftsman that needs hours of 'running in' before it works perfectly.

Wood forms another part of the business, including such treasures as a stock of trees cut 30 years ago. The shop itself is named after Germany's oldest native tree. This appreciation of both quality and style makes sure Holzapfel's cutting edge is always properly seasoned.

Above *This axe has been made by hand by a blacksmith in Sweden. His initials can be seen at the top of the blade, near the handle.*

Below *Alexis Zweifler favours knives made by Japanese master craftsmen, whose tradition was honed by supplying Samurai warriors.*

PAOLO BRANDOLISIO

Gondola oar locks

FOUNDED By Giuseppe Carli, the last focole mastercraftsman
OWNER Paolo Brandolisio, Carli's pupil
SPECIALITIES Gondola oar locks (focole) and oars
ADDRESS/PHONE Castello 4725, 30122 Venice, Italy; tel: (00 39) 041 522 4155
NEAR St Mark's Square
OPENING HOURS Monday to Friday 9am–1pm and 3pm–7pm

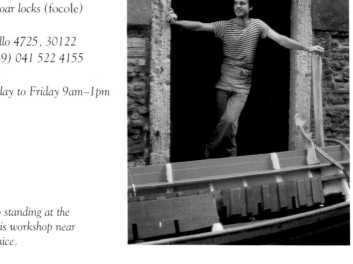

Right Paolo Brandolisio standing at the canalside front door of his workshop near St Mark's Square in Venice.

Like most workshops, there is pop rattling around the radio and every corner is filled with useful clutter in jumbled strata. The pictures on the walls are of the Pope, a football team, a Canaletto and a couple of 'lovelies'. There are, however, only two workshops of this kind left, for Paolo Brandolisio specializes in gondola oar locks, or *focole*, as they are called in Venice.

At one side of the workshop is a doorway onto a canal, framing the milky green water and the soft, pinky-red of the brick outside. This used to be, and still is for some, the front door. The place was previously owned by the late, great master of the craft, Giuseppe Carli. Paolo Brandolisio came to Carli's workshop when he was 14, bringing with him his

first attempt at an oar lock. The master took a good look, said, 'It's beautiful, but...', gave a few tips and encouraged him to make another. When it emerged that Paolo did not have another piece of wood, Carli gave him one, and the apprenticeship began.

The oar-lock design has evolved over centuries of use and the sophisticated shape allows the gondolier to manoeuvre his craft using a single oar placed in eight positions. The oar both pushes the gondola forward and acts as a rudder. A study has shown that three people and the weight of the boat can be propelled with the same energy that it takes a man to walk.

Beyond the efficacy of the design, *focole* are beautiful objects in their own

right; their curves and hooks resembling natural forms that have been scooped and shaped by the elements. In fact, one of Carli's oar locks is on display as a sculpture in the Metropolitan Museum in New York.

Following the age-old practice of the workshop, Paolo puts each *focole* in a special vice, made of wood rather than metal, so that its gentle grip does not mark the oar lock, and he can work on it from all angles. Such is the art of his craft.

PLASTEN

Plastic

FOUNDED *1952 by Olle and Nelly Wernfeld*
OWNER *Vanilla Dahlstrand*
SPECIALITIES *Plastic materials and objects*
ADDRESS/PHONE *St Eriksgata 70, 11320
Stockholm, Sweden; tel/fax: (00 46) 8 34 16 50*
NEAR *Bus route 47 on Vasastan island;
Marianne's Fisk Och Delikatessen
(see pages 24–25)*
OPENING HOURS *Tuesday to Friday
11am–6pm; Saturday 11am–3pm*

On one wall of Plasten are framed
photographs, a tribute to the shop's
founders. Olle and Nelly Wernfeld set
up the business during the 1950s to sell
all kinds of plastic goods, including their
own classic designs for items such as
children's overalls and hanging holdalls.

Vanilla was born in the same year
as the business. She used to visit the
Wernfelds to buy props when she was
working as a stage manager and director
in the theatre. Then she became a
single mother and needed undramatic
working hours just at the point when
the shop and its stock came up for sale.
When she bought Plasten, it was as
much to keep the classic designs going
as anything else.

In one sense, the shop is a tribute to
the Wernfelds, selling materials that are
mostly from the 1950s, '60s and '70s,
but Plasten is also full of a retro-funky
splendour, with its swinging shower
curtains, bright hanging pocket holders,
peg-bags, loo-paper straps and gold dog
jackets. You smile – and then you buy.

Left *A young customer
stands in the doorway
of Plasten – suitably
kitted out in plastic.*

Younger shoppers simply regard the '50s and '60s as hip; others customers are pre-ironic. At the back is a row of frilly capes, now used mostly for dying hair at home, but one or two old-fashioned customers still put them on to keep their clothes spotless when brushing their hair.

One of the regular customers is a man in his eighties who favours designs with roses and visits the shop twice a year from southern Sweden. He once showed Vanilla a picture of his house, a plastic paradise full of furnishings from a time when the fabric represented modernity.

Plastic is past its prime and the range of styles and colours produced has dwindled. The shop itself has a shelf life: when the old stock is used up, it will turn into a museum, or close.

Above *Two swinging peg bags that are part of Plasten's retro-funky stock. They have more than a hundred different kinds of oil-cloth to cover tables and such gems as genuine 1960s pack-a-hats.*

Below *Vanilla became a shop-owner partly to be able to look after her son when she became a single mother.*

JAMES BOWDEN & SONS
AND WEBBER & SONS

Hardware shops

JAMES BOWDEN & SONS
FOUNDED *1862 by James Bowden*
OWNERS *The fourth generation, brothers*
Colin and Peter Smith
SPECIALITIES *Hardware, gumboots,*
outdoor clothes and Moorland equipment
ADDRESS/PHONE *The Square, Chagford,*
Devon TQ13 8AH; tel: 01647 433271,
fax: 01647 433114
NEAR *Dartmoor; the A30*
OPENING HOURS *Monday to Saturday*
9am–5.30pm

WEBBER AND SONS
FOUNDED *1898 by Gideon Webber*
OWNER *Gideon's grandson Eric, his wife Eileen*
and their children Chris, Roderic and Elaine
SPECIALITIES *Hardware, cookware,*
giftware, outdoor clothing
ADDRESS/PHONE *46-48 The Square,*
Chagford, Devon TQ13 8AQ;
tel/fax: 01647 432213
NEAR *Dartmoor; the A30*
OPENING HOURS *Monday to Saturday*
8am–5.30pm

Above *The welly room in Bowden's. Sizes range from children's size three to adults' size 13.*

Left *The garden section of Bowden & Sons, with the shop's museum at the back. One room is filled with boxes bearing labels like 'Domes of Silence', 'vine eyes', 'rising butts' and 'tap swirls'.*

For more than a hundred years, two hardware shops have sat on one side of the market square in the Devon town of Chagford (population: 1,500), owned for all this time by two families. Most of their business is now from visitors, drawn to the town partly by these old-fashioned shops. They even take out joint advertisements. If you can't find something in one, it is bound to be in the other.

When the two families meet socially, talking shop is considered taboo, but in a small community some crossovers are inevitable. Angela Smith used to work for Webber's until she married Colin, joint owner of Bowden's. 'She never mentions anything about their stock, not even today,' says Colin, who has not been into Webber's for some time, '– except to say, "It's ever so tidy".'

Locals agree, saying that you can look around the more apparent order of Webber's but, in a hurry, you should go straight to the counter of Bowden's and inquire. If you can remember the name of the item that is: the shops stock tens of thousands of lines from hundreds of producers.

For most, however, the wandering rummage is all part of the experience. Webber's sells everything from a single screw to four aliens in an egg and has a greater range of cookware and giftware; Bowden's, a browser's paradise of 'thingummies' or 'whatjamaflips', has a museum of the 'whatsits' of the past .

T'MANNETJE

Bicycles

FOUNDED *1984 as a repair shop; 1995 as a bicycle salon by Jan Willem Deymann*

OWNER *Jan Willem Deymann*

SPECIALITIES *Maker, seller and repairer of customized bicycles*

ADDRESS/PHONE *Shop: Frans Halsstraat 26A, 1072 BR Amsterdam, Netherlands; postal address: Quellijnstraat 48, 1072 XT Amsterdam, Netherlands; tel: (00 31) 20 679 21 39*

INTERNET *www.menbike.nl*

NEAR *The Rijksmuseum; the Van Gogh Museum; De Taart van m'n Tante cake shop (see pages 60–61)*

MAIL ORDER *Delivery abroad by arrangement*

OPENING HOURS *Monday to Friday 9am–6pm; Saturday 9am–5pm*

Greater Amsterdam has a million people and two million bicycles. Young women, perched behind their boyfriends, sail like swans beside the canals; doctors and police officers cycle as the quickest way of getting around. This shop began as a repairs workshop specializing in old delivery bikes for itinerant squatters, until Jan Willem Deymann took it over, after working for 22 years as a child psychologist.

His ideas, implemented with an engineer called Michael Kemper, satisfy many different needs and desires, and take into account comfort, durability and style. Parents can take up to four children to school in a tricycle called a 'Filipack' or transport shopping and a toddler in an updated delivery bike called a 'Filibus'.

Right *Bicycles, small dogs and children are how you meet people in the street, says Jan Willem Deymann, the former child psychologist turned bicycle inventor who owns this exceptional shop in Amsterdam.*

Left
Nineteenth-century Russian chandeliers and hi-tech lights illuminate the salon. The bikes are made on site and adapted to customers' needs as necessary.

A restaurateur uses his to cart two boxes of fish from the market each day. One bike carries a wheelchair, another has palm brakes and a small motor for the bad days of Multiple Sclerosis sufferers. 'When people ride my bikes they look beautiful,' says Jan Willem; the vehicle becomes the talking point, not the disability.

Two 19th-century Russian chandeliers and strings of hi-tech lights symbolize how the shop combines old-fashioned class with a progressive edge.

Jan Willem designed a vehicle for a homeless person, partly to stir up debate. Yet he also has models that could slide down a catwalk, such as 'The Italian', inspired by a book on 1930s' cycle couriers, and 'The Pedersen', designed more than a hundred years ago and once issued to the British Army (scooped-down handlebars make room for a machine gun). Jan Willem is interested in practicalities as well as style: to keep the masterpieces safe, T'Mannetje also sells an unbreakable chain, known simply as 'The Beast'.

POLLOCK'S TOY MUSEUM

Toy theatres & toys

FOUNDED 1955 by Marguerite Fawdry.
*The original toy theatre business was started
by John Redington in c.1850*
OWNER *Pollock's Toy Museum
Educational Trust*
SPECIALITIES *Victorian toy theatres and
plays; new toys from around the world*
ADDRESS/PHONE *1 Scala Street, London
W1P 1LT; tel: 020 7636 3452*
E-MAIL/INTERNET *toytheatres@hotmail.com
www.pollocks.cwc.net*
NEAR *Goodge Street Underground*
MAIL ORDER *Theatres and plays
(list available); toys sent, plus cost of p&p*
OPENING HOURS *Monday to Saturday
10am–5pm*

Pollock's Toy Museum is housed in a
former electrician's premises that was
abandoned in the Blitz. Motoring posters
from the 1930s and the chipped brown
varnish on the ceiling add to the shop's
remarkable time-warp frisson.

The shop is named after Benjamin
Pollock, a celebrated seller of toy theatres
who was himself a bit of a curiosity;
trips to his Hoxton premises were an
adventure. He died in 1937, and his
stock was discovered in storage during
the 1950s by Marguerite Fawdry when
she was searching for some wires for
her son's stage. She bought everything:
boxfuls and boxfuls and boxfuls. One
theory has it that her interest in toys
stems from her Catholic childhood:
she was made to give up her own to
the needy.

In the first room are found Pollock's
play sheets and wooden theatres,
complete with trapdoors for the sudden
appearances of demon kings and
fairy queens. Toy theatres did not
patronise or preach morals to Victorian
children but allowed them to revel in
melodrama. Barry, who looks after the
theatres, will explain how they work
with suitable aplomb.

In the second room are new toys
from all over the world, most just as
appealing to adults as to children. 'I only
buy things that I like,' said the manager,

Left *Pollock's was originally housed in Covent
Garden until it moved to these premises, once
owned by an electrician who left during the
Blitz. The toy theatres are in one room, the new
toys in another, and the museum is above.*

Below *A roomful of Victorian toy theatres in the toy museum above the shop.*

Gay Warden as she showed me a tiny wire Elvis Presley with a waggling knee and a wax bird warbler from Morocco. The tabletops of small toys could fill stockings or act as desk distractors.

At the other end of the price list are limited-edition teddy bears sought out by enthusiasts known as 'arctophiles'. Gay occasionally gets phone calls from banks interested in the bears as investments; at the other end of the sentimentality scale are the people who ask her to poke holes in plastic bags so the bears can breathe.

The rest of the building houses a delightful museum. For an entrance fee, you can wind your way up the wooden stairs into the eaves to look at a collection of toys. The whole place is a magic box that conjures up a thousand childhoods from the past – including your own.

AU GRAND RASOIR

Blades

FOUNDED *1821 by Alfonse Jamart*
OWNER *Owned by the Cielen family since 1929*
SPECIALITIES *Knives, razors, scissors; badger-hair shaving brushes; workshop for grinding and repairs*
ADDRESS/PHONE *7 rue de l'Hôpital, 1000 Brussels, Belgium; tel/fax: (00 32) 2 512 49 62*
NEAR *Gare Centrale; Grand Place; Wittamer's cake shop (see pages 58–59)*
OPENING HOURS *Monday to Saturday 9.30am–6.30pm*

Right *The shop has an eye-catching window display, showing off some of the 2,500 blades.*

Left *Just a short walk from the Grand Place in Brussels, Au Grand Rasoir is an old-fashioned shop run by dedicated specialists who believe in quality and care.*

Right *Shaving brushes such as these are made from the finest, softest hairs from the badgers' stomachs.*

The eighties were the dog days of disposable gimmicks, but Monsieur Cielen now sees a return to quality – *les beaux et les bons* – and customers visiting Au Grand Rasoir want objects that last. There has even been a return to cut-throat razors.

With a windowful of gleaming blades, it is the sort of place that people remember and visit more than once. Madame Cielen once called her husband over to meet a customer who had last been there decades before, during the city's liberation in 1944. 'Are you American?' M Cielen asked. The man drew himself up to his full height, went outside and pointed to a chauffeur-driven silver Rolls Royce. 'I am English,' he replied, 'and so is my car.'

M Cielen learned his trade from his grandparents, and remembers travelling around factories and one-man workshops from the age of six. This is a specialists' world, there are 250 different kitchen knives, depending on whether you want to filet a sole or stab off a hunk of Parmesan. It took many years to learn the details of every trade the shop supplies.

Only the Cielens serve in the shop and they take care of the customers at all stages of a transaction. Knives are sent in for sharpening by individuals, businesses and surgeons.

As well as blades, Au Grand Rasoir also offers a range of badger-hair shaving brushes, on display in a case by the front entrance. The fair ones are the best quality because they are made of the finer hairs from the animals' fronts rather than the coarser back bristles.

A good game is to try to guess the use of some of the 2,500 objects on display. A pair of scissors with blades as long as a small child's legs turns out to be for wallpaper. A small pair with a slight curve is designed to trim the hairs on a dog's paws. A sturdy blade with a brush at the end is clearly for mushroom picking, but how many would know the purpose of that fearsome-looking instrument used to crack sea-urchin shells?

EL REY DE LA MAGIA

Magic

FOUNDED *1881 by Joaquim Partagàs*
OWNERS: *Josep Martínez Augusti and Rosa Maria Llop*
SPECIALITIES *Magic tricks and joke items*
ADDRESS/PHONE *Carrer Princesa 11, 08003 Barcelona, Spain; tel: (00 34) 93 319 7393, fax: (00 34 93) 319 39 20*
E-MAIL/INTERNET *reymagia@arrakis.es www.arrakis.es/-reymagia/*
NEAR *Metro Jaume 1*
OPENING HOURS *Monday to Wednesday, Friday and Saturday 10am–2pm and 5pm–8pm; Thursday 10am–2pm*

The entrance to El Rey de la Magia is more than slightly mysterious, with windows cloaked in curtains and no knob on the door. You burst in uncertainly, unsure what to expect. The first couple of times, I found it empty, apart from a disembodied hand holding back a curtain. Then a small, dark woman stepped out from nowhere and stood still and silent. Black and white photographs of famous magicians and hypnotists watched from the walls with hooded, mesmerizing stares. They were all customers, too.

The shop was opened in 1881 by Joaquim Partagàs, who made his own tricks, some of which can be glimpsed on the shelves. It was taken on by Charles Bucheli, another magician and

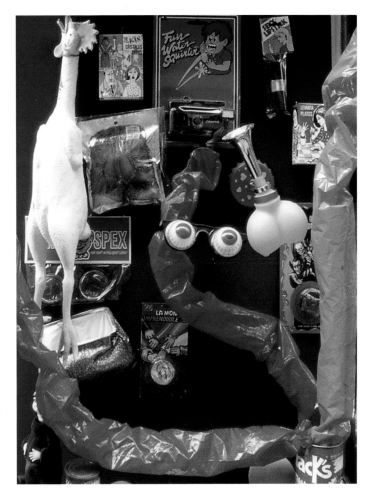

Right *A display of jokes in a cabinet on the outside of El Rey de la Magia.*

Left *El Rey de la Magia is a mysterious, entertaining magic shop in Barcelona that has been owned by three generations of magicians.*

customer. In a photograph on the wall he looks surprisingly normal, despite spikes through his cheek and chin.

The shop eventually passed into the hands of the current owners, Josep and Rosa, also former customers and magicians. The couple had turned from acting to magic by forming a company, La Capsca Màgica (the Magic Box) in 1977, viewing magic as another form of expression, like dance. They wanted to continue all the business' best traditions.

Today, magicians visit El Rey de la Magia for customized tricks; curious tourists gaze at the walls and go away with postcards or a joke (they sell the usual squirty cameras, hairy ears and chilli tea-bags). A bunch of flowers may spring from a curtain with the wave of a wand; perhaps there will be a trick with hankerchieves, balls or cards. Sleight of hand, mirrors or demonic devices? Your eyes try to pin down the magic, but in the end you are inexplicably beguiled by the abaracadabra of the magician's art.

LARCH COTTAGE NURSERIES

Plants & pizzas

FOUNDED *1985 by Peter and Briony Stott*

OWNERS *Peter and Briony Stott*

SPECIALITIES *Herbaceous plants, slab stained-glass*

ADDRESS/PHONE *Larch Cottage Nurseries, Melkinthorpe, Penrith, Cumbria CA10 2DR; tel: 01931 712404, fax: 01931 712727*

E-MAIL *briony@larchcottage.freeserve.co.uk*

NEAR *About 10 minutes' drive from Penrith and the M6*

MAIL ORDER *Catalogue available, next-day deliveries*

OPENING HOURS *Monday to Sunday 10am–7pm; closed two weeks over Christmas*

Peter Stott does not like walls.

Sometimes he knocks them down; sometimes he builds them ready-ruined, in the spirit of the 18th-century Romantic garden, where they act as prompts for the imagination rather than rigid divisions. At the base of Peter's feelings about walls is a sense that he does not like containment, and Larch Cottage is a place that, delightfully, breaks boundaries.

To start with, it is a nursery that specializes in unusual herbaceous plants. Gardeners come for rarities. Other people, who know nothing whatsoever

Left *Some people spend all day at Larch Cottage, treating it like a garden instead of a nursery, and punctuating the day with delicious food from the café.*

Right *Garden sculptures and urns. The nursery is co-owned by a garden architect who is interested in all parts of the garden, not just plants, and who makes slab stained glass.*

about horticulture, will happily treat the place like a garden, wandering through the different textures and shades, the jumble of statues and the stained-glass windows that harmonize with the colours of the plants as they change through the seasons. Beyond the nursery are medieval strip fields, protected by a preservation order and bordered by

hedges that swerve sinuously in an echo of the turns of yesteryear's oxen plough.

Larch Cottage is not just about plants. The main building has a wood-fired pizza oven and a café with delicious cakes, espresso and honest, fresh food. It is a genuinely welcoming place, and not just tagged on to the nursery to make money – the prices are amazingly good value.

Left *One of Peter's ready-ruined walls and some of the plants on sale.*

Right *The view over the nursery across to the hills. The shot was taken from a building put up by the nursery's owner – the cause of an epic victory over local planning authorities.*

That gives you strength: it's an ideal. I wouldn't do what I am doing for money: it wouldn't be worth it.'

The week after the inquiry, Peter went to Italy for the first time and fell in love. He connected to the place with an instant, profound, visceral and spiritual attachment. Two weeks later he returned, this time with his family. It is hard to believe that Larch Cottage was created before he and Briony started to spend time in Italy. You sit on a balcony, surrounded by flowers and Italian opera eating a meal that has the style and spirit of al fresco dining and looking across at mountains. Is this Cumbria or Umbria?

Peter was a ballet and modern dancer in London before coming home to use his dancer's balance to perform gravity-defying feats as a tree-surgeon and getting into garden design, principally through garden architecture. Briony studied botany at university before becoming a teacher and latterly setting up the nursery. Their next plan is an accessible arts space in another building.

Twice a year, at Christmas and in the summer, Peter and Briony hold parties for the village, as a thank-you-cum-get-together. Larch Cottage is a business, yet it is also full of a purpose that is not about getting and spending, but a far richer, more dynamic brew of new hybrids, cross-fertilization and growth.

The café resides in a building Peter designed and put up himself, breaking the rules of the local planning authority officials who ordered him to take it down again within three months.

After a £70,000 battle (suppliers gave him time to pay, locals volunteered whole-hearted support), there was a packed meeting for the public inquiry. An inspector came back in a record seven days saying it was the epitome of vernacular architecture using local materials. The spirit of the law won an unequivocal victory over the letter of the rule book.

'Your vision is more important than most other things,' Peter says. 'It is not just to make money; it's because you have a belief in what you are doing.

SCENTS AND STITCHES

BRILMUSEUM

Spectacles

FOUNDED *Opened as an opticians in 1620; current shop in 1996 by Jan and Mÿke Teunissen*

OWNER *Mÿke Teunissen*

SPECIALITIES *20th-century spectacles*

ADDRESS/PHONE *Gasthuismolensteeg 7, 1016 AM Amsterdam, Netherlands; tel: (00 31) 20 4212 414*

NEAR *Anne Frank's house; the Golden Bend; the Dam*

OPENING HOURS *Wednesday to Saturday 12pm–5.30pm*

Right *The exterior of the Brilmuseum, a shop that stocks new spectacles from past decades.*

The collection of specs on show at the Brilmuseum was put together over 35 years by Jan Teunissen, who travelled around Europe picking up the unsold stock of closing opticians. Everything on sale is new, yet old. Modern designers copy old frames, but here you can buy the real thing at a fraction of the price, whether you are after Schubert or Clark Kent, maxi-chic or Dame Edna.

Mÿke Teunissen spent ten years on her father's pilgrimage, as well as studying fashion and architecture. It was while restoring this building, which used to house one of the oldest opticians in Amsterdam, that she formed the idea of turning it into a shop and museum for her father's collection.

The shop is a 'museum-for-sale' of 20th-century frames. Its top two floors are a real museum that spans over 700 years of specs. 'Look, look, look!' the whole place says. Look at the Elton John extravaganzas and the massive wink glasses! Look at the way frames got bigger as skirts got shorter! Look at the jokes staring at you from the walls and the ceiling! (And watch your feet on what must be some of the most treacherous stairs in the city.)

Jan Teunissen died shortly after the shop opened, but his words and ideas are everywhere. An optician, he wrote, is a physician, technician and fashion designer. The museum charts the running debate between oval and round frames, the coolest shades of the 20th century and the way spectacles developed with printing. By the way: it took a remarkably long time before ears were used as 'hooks'; until then, the arms were simply stuck into one's wig.

Left *One of the Brilmuseum's rooms, where visual jokes on the ceiling and walls overlook quirky and informative displays of spectacles.*

Right *The shop and museum show off some of the trendiest shades of the 20th century.*

PHARMACEUTICA DI SANTA MARIA NOVELLI

Perfumes & toiletries

FOUNDED *1221 by Dominican monks, who ran it until it was ceded to Cesare Stefani in 1866*
OWNER *The Stefani family, eighth generation*
SPECIALITIES *Toiletries, eau-de-Colognes, Santa Maria Novella water*
ADDRESS/PHONE *Via della Scala 16n, Florence, Italy; tel: (00 39) 055 230 2883/2649/2437, fax: (00 39) 055 288 658; London branch: 117 Walton Street, London, SW3; tel: 020 7460 6600*
NEAR *Piazza Santa Maria Novella*
OPENING HOURS *Monday 3.30pm–7.30pm; Tuesday to Saturday 9.30am–7.30pm*

Below *The back room of the pharmacy, and the many treasures in its glass-fronted cabinets.*

Customers leave the hot Florence street to bathe in the welcome chill of the marble entrance of the Pharmaceutica di Santa Maria Novelli, where celestial classical music and fragrances are carried on the cool air. The sounds of the till and the rustling tourists are almost incongruous in this old pharmacy, which has managed to preserve its cloistered feel despite falling into secular hands when Napoleon confiscated church property in 1866, and the building passed into the hands of the nephew of the last Dominican director. Now, soldiers exercise in the courtyard, beyond the walls of bottles.

The fragrances, essences, pomades, liqueurs and toiletries have been the

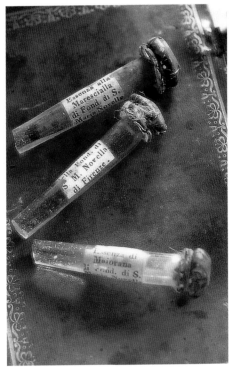

Above *Old phials are some of the countless curiosities to look at in the pharmacy of Santa Maria Novelli.*

Above *Perfumes in a cupboard in the front room of the Pharmaceutica, which is a celebrated example of neo-Gothic decoration.*

same for centuries, since monks first devised the mixtures to care for the sick from the 13th century onwards. Santa Maria Novella water, with its bergamot and citrus notes, was created for Catherine de Medici and went with her to France and then to Cologne, where it became the original eau-de-Cologne.

Other fragrances include straw, moss and tobacco as well as magnolia, rose and orange blossom. The Aromatic Vinegar is also called Water of the Seven Thieves; the story goes that a gang of seven grave robbers used it against corpse stench and infection,

each knowing just one ingredient so they could not betray the others.

Visitors were received in the middle room, with hot chocolate or a sample of one of the drinkable specialities such as rhubarb elixir. The back room contains endless bygone curiosities, such as a thermometer that looks like a fairground ride and an advertisement for an inhalation apparatus.

The shop is favoured by American women draped in floppy hats, flowing garments and a studied languor, like actresses in a Merchant Ivory film who just *might* get an attack of the vapours.

BRIC-A-BRAC 1 AND BRIC-A-BRAC 2

Art deco objects & bric-à-brac

FOUNDED *1991 by Milos Gavrilovic and Sonja Popovic*

OWNER *Milos Gavrilovic and Sonja Popovic*

SPECIALITIES *Bric-à-Brac 1: a collector's cave of well-made, interesting small objects; Bric-à-Brac 2: art deco objects*

ADDRESS *shared postal address Bric-à-Brac 1 and Bric-à-Brac 2, Tynsk 7, Prague 1, Czech Republic; Bric-à-Brac 1: tel: (00 42 0) 2 232 6484; Bric-à-Brac 2: tel: (00 42 0) 2 248 15763; shared fax: (00 42 0) 606 873 955*

E-MAIL *spopovic@iol.cz*

NEAR *Old Town Square*

OPENING HOURS *Monday to Sunday 10am–6pm*

The Czech Republic, its history layered with periods of affluence and hardship, provides rich pickings for seekers of the second-hand. Well-made goods bought in the good times were kept through the bad; now, in the shiny, post-communist world, it is time to sell. Visitors splash about in a river of lovely old objects. Bric-à-Brac 1 and 2 stand out among the many shops of their kind in Prague because of a genuine love for the articles.

Milos Gavrilovic and Sonja Popovic have one large, light shop, Bric-à-Brac 2, that is a haven for art deco and arranged like an enormous, intricate still life: a row of evening bags hanging on a line like bobbing apples, pearls on seashells, elegant irons, wooden toy boats, perfume sprayers, cameras, Mosser crystal, little

Left *The exterior of Bric-à-Brac 1, a rich cave of bits and bobs in a quiet street in Prague. Its sister shop, Bric-à-Brac 2, is round the corner.*

Right *A 90-year-old woman brought in this sequined costume: she had made it herself for her trapeze act. She decided to sell to Bric-à-Brac 2 because she liked the shop.*

boxes and records of operas. Customers expecting to rifle through mere *stuff* instead regard each piece with respect.

The other shop, Bric-à-Brac 1, is a dim, exciting cave of bits and bobs. In the middle sits a put-together throne-of-a-chair that is a still point in a shifting, sifting world. This room is the haunt of collectors, those avid accumulators of scales, thimbles, cups, egg cups, eye-wash cups – anything – who are hooked on a theme, often for a reason long forgotten. Milos has a friend who comes in for shoe horns, which he began collecting because his surname means 'shoe horn'.

Right *Small bangles are among the piles of objects that can be found in both shops. Bric-à-Brac 2 deals with more decorative art-deco objects, while Bric-à-Brac 1 is a mass of bits and pieces.*

(Later he discovered the family was more likely named after a bay in Estonia, but by this time his father was caught too.)

Milos has a passion for bits and pieces. While other dealers make a tidy profit on a single chest of drawers, he becomes absorbed by a box of watches, taking them apart and examining the beauty of their hand-crafted mechanisms. It is the small objects, made to last, that catch his eye at the markets and auctions. Perhaps a necklace of 1930s crystal beads. Perhaps a fountain-pen. Perhaps a silver scalloped scoop with holes that once served ice for smart drinks. 'I'm not destroying, I'm not producing,' he says. 'I'm just giving second life to things that would be discarded.'

Milos and Sonja came to Prague from the former Yugoslavia. He is Serbian, she Croatian. They lived in Belgrade. One night in 1991 they watched a general on the television, saw the expression on his face, packed the car and left the country the next day.

At first, Sonja, who had worked as a writer, made and sold clothes. Milos kept a personal collection of objects in the shop for people to look at while they waited. Everything was stolen in a break-in during the first month. 'I learned that it's not too healthy to be connected to things,' he said. Beautiful objects now flow through their hands, shops and home. Sonja sometimes dreams of an uncluttered Japanese space.

Left *The interior of Bric-à-Brac 1, which is situated in a building where harmonicas were once made.*

Right *Old irons in Bric-à-Brac 2.*

Below *Puppets hanging up in Bric-à-Brac 2. The shop has everything from hats and handbags, old crystal and opera records to bits of kitchenware and houseware.*

V V ROULEAUX

Ribbons

FOUNDED *1990 by Anabelle Lewis*

OWNER *Anabelle Lewis*

SPECIALITIES *Ribbons and trimmings*

ADDRESS/PHONE *54 Sloane Square, London SW1W 8AX; tel: 020 7730 3125, fax: 020 7730 3468; and at 6 Marylebone High Street, London W1*

MAIL ORDER *Minimum order of £10, £2.50 for p&p*

NEAR *Sloane Square Underground; John Sandoe's bookshop (see pages 138–139)*

OPENING HOURS *Monday to Saturday 9.30am–6pm; Wednesday 9.30am–6.30pm*

The downstairs room of V V Rouleaux is a cross between a fantasy sewing box and a rainbow factory. Spools display 5,000 ribbons of every shade and texture: organza as fluttery as butterfly wings, subtle antique fabrics, rich velvets and girlish ginghams. The sheer gorgeousness is set off by the stark metal shop fittings that were once part of a milking parlour belonging to the owner's father.

Anabelle Lewis set up the business in 1990 after noticing a lack of ribbons in beautiful colours, and because she was tired of getting up early as a florist.

Right *Gorgeous hues and textures among the thousands of colours and styles at V V Rouleaux. The shop was set up when the owner noticed the poor range of ribbons generally on offer.*

Left *The front room of the shop, which contains trimmings for furniture. Downstairs there is a roomful of ribbons and other trimmings.*

Selling flowers taught her that the single bloom is left alone; banks of colour sell. If something is not available, the business makes it. Around 30 per cent of the stock is specially commissioned from workshops all over the world.

Anabelle's enthusiasm has influenced style and fashion pundits. Look through a rack of magazines and you start to notice the number of ribbons weaving their way through the pages, be it sofa covers, bikinis or a bondage-look fashion shoot for the magazine *Dazed and Confused*. International designers may initially schedule a short meeting but stay for hours thinking up ideas – 'creative wholesaling', Anabelle calls it.

Among the more contemporary uses for ribbons are the looped crosses that signal awareness of breast cancer and HIV and AIDS: it was V V Rouleaux that provided the yellow ribbons for the Hostage campaign that first popularized the idea. Among the more traditional uses are military colours for medals, made by a specialist weaver in Coventry. When I last visited, the Secretary of the Whippet Society had been in, and followers of fashion were looking for feathers for their jeans.

CASA CRESPO

Espadrilles

FOUNDED *1863 by Gregorio Crespo*
OWNER *The fourth generation, Maxi and Gloria Garbayo*
SPECIALITIES *Espadrilles*
ADDRESS/PHONE *Calle del Divino Pastor 29, 28004 Madrid, Spain; tel: (00 34) 91 521 5654*
NEAR *Bilbao metro*
OPENING HOURS *Monday to Friday 10am–1.30pm, 4.30pm–8pm*

Right *A front window showing some of the 15 styles of espadrille stocked in the shop.*

There are woven bags, coils of rope and brushes made from natural plant fibres, but mostly Casa Crespo sells espadrilles in 30 colours and 15 styles. Rainbow stripes stuck to the shelves display the colours of the stock ranging from sunshine-yellow, turquoise and bubblegum-pink to subtler shades such as soft cherry-red and mushroom. The shoes themselves are stacked up in pairs with their white-stitched toes placed together so they look like piles of smiles.

Espadrilles were first used by sailors and farmers as conveniently lightweight canvas shoes; they were taken up by the fashionable Riviera set in the Twenties, their popularity boosted by such devotees as Picasso. The Queen of Spain and her offspring are among the regulars who turn up at this shop every year when summer comes. The floorboards are like sand that has been ridged over the decades by the seasonal ebb and flow of customers.

The shoes are made in the northern Rioja region, in workshops where some of the seamstresses have been with the firm for decades. The shoes reflect that expertise: they are beautifully made, with hand stitching and reinforced toes. A small rack of wooden rods on one side of the shop is used to push into the ends of the shoes to make the fit more comfortable when customers try them on. The sizes range from the small to the large, from 20 to 46. Casa Crespo also welcomes children with a bowl of sweets – as colourful and alluring as the merchandise itself.

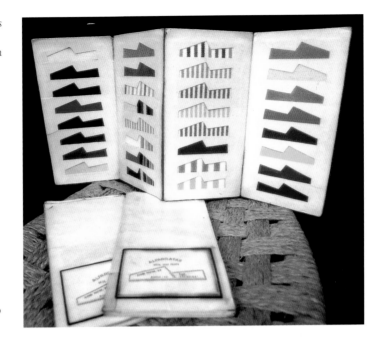

Below *Some of the 30 colours of shoes on sale, ranging from sunny yellow to subtle browns.*

M G W SEGAS

Canes

FOUNDED *1984 by Miguel and Gilbert Segas*

OWNER *Miguel and Gilbert Segas*

SPECIALITIES *An astonishing range of canes of all descriptions*

ADDRESS/PHONE *34 Passage Jouffroy, 75009 Paris, France; tel: (00 33 1) 47 70 89 65, fax: (00 33 1) 48 00 08 24*

INTERNET *www.antique-expo.com/mgwsegas www.surfrance.com/mgw_segas*

NEAR *Métro Rue Montmartre; Musée Grevin; Chartier restaurant*

OPENING HOURS *Monday to Saturday 11.30am–6.30pm*

M G W Segas has the dramatic panache of the stage. The exterior is topped by a vast pair of horns, and the shop's interior is a reassembly of stage sets. Miguel, one of the owners, dances around in a flourish, stage right, stage left; downstairs, demonstrating a dandy's dawdle; upstairs, opening a drawer to reveal a Belle Epoque flagellation device. He and his brother Gilbert were actors in their father's theatre in Rouen until it closed. They became fascinated by the canes in the redundant prop department and collected and exhibited before eventually opening a shop in this elegant Parisian arcade.

A hundred years ago, the cane was the sartorial equivalent of the tie: a fashion accessory that was an opportunity for display. A gentleman might change his cane four or five times a day according to the time, place and occasion. (Perhaps the tie will, in time, go the same way as the cane.)

There are, Miguel explains, four types. First, the canes that have carved and polished decorative heads – perhaps an eagle with glinting eyes or a monkey with a lolling tongue. Second, there are ones that show off different materials, be it backbone, hippopotamus skin, glass like spun sugar or thousands of little discs of newspaper stuck on a spike.

Third, the popular art decorations: canes whittled with carvings in the trenches of the First World War, for example.

Finally – and most entertaining of all – are device canes with an ingenuity that makes James Bond look a touch 'Blue Peter'. A debonair 1930s' picnic cane turns into a coathanger to swing a blazer from a branch. Others double as cigarette holders, artists' easels, sword-sticks, knife-fork-and-toothpick-sticks. Elsewhere you can find canes that turned into ear trumpets or pipes, canes with special pull-out maps, canes for painters

Left *The shop is situated in the elegant Jouffroy arcade in the ninth arrondissement of Paris. The arcade contains many absorbing specialist shops. An eye-catching window display makes M G W Segas unmistakable.*

Below *Miguel and Gilbert Segas among their astonishing range of canes. The brothers were actors in their father's private theatre until it closed down, and they used the canes in the prop department to start off their collection.*

and canes for fighters. Ladies would carry canes containing miniature powder puffs or tiny clocks that rewound with a twist of the top. There were even subterfuge political canes with subtly shaped handles to cast shadow profiles of Louis XVI.

M G W Segas is a lively shop, full of fun and laughter. It is only when you leave the premises to walk away down the covered arcade and into the petrol blast of the boulevard outside, that you feel a twinge of regret. Today, these beautiful objects are only to be found in shops or collections, but once they belonged to a sauntering age of elegance – one that existed before the race of mechanical wheels replaced strolling feet and the gentle art of promenading.

Left and right
Some of the decorative cane heads among the thousands that reside at M G W Segas.

KNOPF PAUL

Button shop

FOUNDED *1979 by Paul Knopf*
OWNER *Paul Knopf*
SPECIALITIES *More than a million buttons spanning the 20th century*
ADDRESS/PHONE *Zossener Strasse 10, 10961 Berlin; tel: (00 49 0) 30 692 1212, fax: (00 49 0) 30 694 1500*
NEAR *Gneisenau U-Bahn 7 in west Kreuzberg*
OPENING HOURS *Tuesday and Friday 9am–6pm; Wednesday and Thursday 2pm–6pm*

Above *Owner Paul Knopf (his name translates as 'Paul Button') reaching for one of the boxes that contain some of his million buttons.*

A honeycomb of more than a million buttons stretches from floor to ceiling in Knopf Paul. Suddenly, your eye magpies onto the glint of something special: a toggle made of wiring, then an exquisite 1930s' design in black glass, then a plastic flower from the hippy era, then turn-of-the-century painted metal. If you spread out a hundred types, each person would pick out a different favourite, says owner Paul Knopf.

A bearish man with a gentle grace, he pulls out tubes like organ stops. 'They are more than for fixing clothes,' he says. 'They tell you about the history of the time, in their individual style, form, material.' Button-makers used to have one of the longest apprenticeships, along with bookbinders, because they dealt with so many materials. The shop's back rooms are crammed with tools – and more buttons, of course.

Paul started collecting as a child and sold at a market after school. The buttons and jewellery he makes reflect his own times: cufflinks made of old typewriter keys, or a pair of earrings: one the shape of West Germany, the other East.

Customers vary from the young and funky to those who arrive on the annual pilgrimage of the Button Collecting Club of Switzerland. Members of the Berlin league of button-football players spend hours examining backs of buttons to find secret angles for star strikers. Film, theatre and opera designers come to get the last detail right. Kindergarten teachers buy a kilogram of buttons for ten Deutschmarks.

There are often garments spread out on the counters as people try out dozens of kinds of buttons, putting them back in their boxes with the shiny, rapid, clickety-clock of pebbles after a wave.

Above *Knopf's myriad buttons are kept in tubes that slot neatly into converted milk crates.*

Left *The shop stocks buttons made from every sort of material: glass, metal, stone, funky plastic, fine enamel... even teddy-bear eyes.*

HERBORISTERIA DEL REI

Herbal pharmacy

FOUNDED *1823 by Josep Vilá*
OWNER *Trinitat Sabatés*
SPECIALITIES *A pharmacy specializing in herbs and spices*
ADDRESS/PHONE *Carrer del Vidre 1, 08002 Barcelona, Spain; tel/fax: (00 34) 93 318 0512*
NEAR *Plaça Reial and the Ramblas; Liceu metro*
OPENING HOURS *Monday to Saturday 10am–2pm and 5pm–8pm*

The Herboristeria del Rei stayed in the same family for 171 years, until the last owner, Manuela Ballart, died without issue. The back room, its low ceiling a reminder of the smaller generations of the past, still contains her scythe-bladed guillotine – once used to chop herbs but today padlocked to prevent an accident. Manuela's rat-traps hang from the ceiling and the beams are lined with nails on which herbs dry. Another room is a den of scents piled high with boxes of herbs; perforated screens in the door allow the air to circulate and keep the stock cool.

The interior of the shop itself was redecorated in 1860 to celebrate its new status as supplier to the Queen, and these majestic fittings are those visible today. The landscape watercolours on the

Above *This shop, hidden down an alleyway, has a perfectly-preserved exterior and interior from the early 19th century. Through the door you can see the old marble stand that used to hold leeches for treatments.*

Right *Tiny weights on the scales measure out herbs in this early 19th-century pharmacy.*

drawers are so elegant that it is slightly surprising to find ordinary goods inside them. The ceiling is covered in painted glass, apart from a small section that reveals even older decorations. There is a marble fountain that used to blaze with early gas lights. Leeches were kept in the water, ready to be used for treatments.

The name of the shop was changed to reflect its royal status, but in republican times this became politically incorrect; for a while it reverted to its old name in tribute to the 18th-century Swedish botanist and taxonomist Linnaeus. On the door you can see where the shop has dropped and reinstated its royal tag because 'del Rei' has been repainted in plainer letters and the 'herboristeria' is still in gold.

Herbal and other traditional remedies are undergoing quite a revival, but some Catalans have never lost the herbal habit. The bulk of the shop's income is not from tourists but regulars. One customer says that leeches were used in remote villages right up until the middle of the 20th century. Pharmacies and herbalists in general seem to keep going for longer than other small businesses, particularly in Barcelona where there are a large number of old shops still intact. Perhaps pharmacies survive because the shortcomings of human health make for eternally good business.

J M SMITH & SONS

Umbrellas & sticks

FOUNDED *1830 by James Smith*

OWNERS *The fifth generation of family members*

SPECIALITIES *Maker, seller and repairer of umbrellas, sticks, sunshades, crooks and canes*

ADDRESS/PHONE *Hazelwood House, 53 New Oxford Street, London WC1A 1BL; tel: 020 7836 4731, fax: 020 7836 4730*

NEAR *Holborn Underground; the British Museum; Cornelissen's art supplies shop (see pages 138–139)*

MAIL ORDER *Within UK and Ireland, add £8 for each item; overseas orders sent by air and cost added to credit card or invoiced separately*

OPENING HOURS *Monday to Friday 9.30am–5.25pm; Saturday 10am–5.25pm*

J M Smith, a Victorian gem with hundreds of umbrellas and a courteous approach to service, gives customers reason to feel cheerful about the rain. It is lucky that umbrellas are such useful, losable, breakable items, for this provides an excuse to return many times.

The front has gold and red glass advertisements for Tropical Sunshades and Dagger Canes, and the inside is so stuffed with curiosities that it could belong to one of Mary Poppin's uncles; and there is her parrot-headed umbrella, lying on a counter.

The manager thinks rain brings out the essential character of London, with dashing people and reflections on wet pavements. Umbrellas and sticks are also lightning rods for eccentricity, supposedly a British trait. A few years

Left *Part of the front room of the most celebrated umbrella shop in London. At the back you can see part of their collection of umbrella- and stick-related pictures.*

Right *A rack of umbrellas with decorative animal heads.*

back, a man in a broad, black hat and sweeping cloak came into the shop, loomed over an assistant and demanded, 'Has Jesus Christ been in?' 'He doesn't come in every day,' was the reply, without a missed beat. Staff have learned that it is impossible to predict who's who. The manager once approached an old woman, guessing she was off to Bournemouth for a break: it was Borneo, to study orangutans.

On the wall are tribal sticks for various African chiefs, and the shop's collection of umbrella pictures, including a photo of a rainy peace rally in 1914 with Hyde Park draped over in a sea of black umbrellas. While you wait, you can sit on turn-of-the-century bentwood Viennese chairs that used to reside in the family's dining-room, when they lived above the shop.

Left *Drawers of umbrellas waiting to be mended. Smith's has a workshop below the shop, which carries out repairs. The business also makes some of its own stock.*

CLASSIC CRAFTS

LJUNGGRENS PAPPERSHANDEL

Paper

FOUNDED *In 1913 by Selma Ljunggrens; bought and changed by Barbara Bunke in 1989*

OWNER *Barbara Bunke*

SPECIALITIES *Papers from all over the world, hand-made books, sealing wax*

ADDRESS/PHONE *Shop: Köpmangatan 3, Gamla Stan, Stockholm; postal address: Suartmangatan 9, 1129 Stockholm, Sweden; tel: (00 46) 8 676 0383, fax: (00 46) 8 103377*

NEAR *On Gamla Stan (the Old Town) near the Royal Palace, on bus routes 46 and 55*

MAIL ORDER *By arrangement*

OPENING HOURS *Tuesday to Friday 11am–6pm; Saturday 11am–3pm; closed Saturdays in July and August*

Ljunggrens Pappershandel's interior is as exquisite as a landscape under snow, with sheets of paper hanging from the walls like whitened tiles and a pure serenity in every corner. The rusty doors at the back date from to the 14th century, and are transformed by the plain luminosity of the shop to look like textured modern art. There is a calm, slightly muffled atmosphere: a peace of paper.

The finest papers to be found at Ljunggrens include Japanese hand-made sheets, the most delicate weighing just 7.5g per square metre compared to photocopier paper's hefty 80g. Others are strong and flexible enough to use as curtains. In the Far East, paper has been used to make wedding dresses; garments, after all, that you never need to clean.

Above *Some of the shop's hand-made paper. A man who restores pre-1500 books for the Vatican and travels the world in search of materials thought Ljunggrens' was the best selection of paper he had ever seen.*

Left *The shop's owner, Barbara Bunke, and her two immaculate dogs – which are as clean as new paper.*

Below *Ljunggrens' address, written in Barbara's elegant script. She was a graphic designer before becoming a shop owner.*

Barbara Bunke maintains the shop with perfectionism. As a young girl, she collected stationery, making piles of envelopes with the largest at the bottom and the smallest on top, one pile for straight flaps, another for pointed. While working as a graphic designer, she learned how to bind books with her clean, neat fingers. She still screen-prints covers for the shop's hand-made books.

One day, the streets were empty of traffic because cars are banned from Stockholm's old town at certain times. A taxi drew up, and the employees' eyes followed. Their eyes widened when Jackie O stepped out. She looked at the window. (Yes!) She walked away. (No!) She came back. (Yes!) She had admired some cards in the window the night before and made a special trip back; the display had been changed, and at first she hadn't recognized the shop.

Your best customer may be someone who come once a week for decades, or a superstar who drops from the sky.

TADDEI

Leather boxes

FOUNDED *1937 by Otello Taddei*
OWNER *Otello's grandson, Simone Taddei*
SPECIALITIES *Fine leather boxes and desk accessories*
ADDRESS/PHONE *Via Santa Margherita 11, Florence, Italy; tel/fax: (00 39) 055 239 8960*
NEAR *The Duomo*
OPENING HOURS *Monday to Saturday 8am–7.30pm; sometimes closed at lunchtime*

It takes Simone Taddei weeks of patient work, 32 stages in all, to make each leather box that is sold in Taddei. It took 14 years at his father's side to learn the trade, and there are now four generations of knowledge behind the techniques – yet it costs just £20 for one of the smaller boxes. 'You must touch the leather to

Above Simone Taddei in the workshop where he makes leather boxes in 32 painstaking stages. At the back you can see the rack of tools, many of them handed down through the generations of his family.

learn and understand, to build up your experience,' says Simone, who starts around 8am every day and works until 7.30pm (his father used to start at five or six in the morning).

His method evolved from a mixture of trades. Simone's great-grandfather was a shoemaker for Ferragamo; his hammer, a lump of metal attached to the handle by a strap of leather, is still in use today. It was Simone's grandfather who founded the business, after picking up ideas from shoemaking and other leather trades. Each generation has slowly built on this foundation, adding a colour or a shape but always retaining the classic lines that

Above and right
The boxes are strapped into special wooden forms that help to mould their shapes. The outside wood is taken off so the boxes can be polished and removed from the wooden blocks inside.

suited, and still suit, Anglo-Saxon tastes: around 85 per cent of Simone Taddei's customers are British or American. Some are such avid collectors that they have the entire range of around 70 pieces.

To make each box, Simone puts layer upon layer of leather onto wooden forms, with cowhide to give them strength and calfskin for softness on top. He then burnishes and polishes the outside before cutting the boxes off the blocks. The finished product is imbued with a lustrous, deep glow. 'When it is so plain, it has to be perfect,' he says.

Simone worked alongside his father, Giampaolo, until a couple of weeks before the latter's death; then Simone suddenly found himself alone. And he cannot simply take on more staff – they lack the necessary years of experience. Finding custom is not the problem, just keeping up with the demand.

It is an operation almost poignantly at odds with modern commerce.

P C J HAJENIUS

Cigars & pipes

FOUNDED *1826 by Pantaleon Gerhard*
OWNER *Burger, Switzerland*
SPECIALITIES *Cigars, tobacco and pipes*
ADDRESS/PHONE *Rokin 92–96, 1012 KZ Amsterdam, Netherlands; tel: (00 31) 20 623 74 94, fax: (00 31) 20 6387221*
INTERNET *www.hajenius.com*
NEAR *The Dam*
MAIL ORDER *Everywhere in Europe, except the UK and Austria*
OPENING HOURS *Monday 12pm–6pm; Tuesday to Saturday 9.30am–6pm; Thursday 9.30am–9pm; Sunday 12pm–5pm*

Below *The exterior of Hajenius: a beautiful, grand shop with an open-door policy that makes it welcoming as well as luxurious.*

Hajenius is a shop at ease with pleasure. A notice on the door reads, 'Thank-you for smoking.' The heavy doors at the front of the building were propped open a couple of years ago to make the shop literally more accessible, and some people come in briefly just to sniff the perfumed air that is a cross between silken hay and golden peppers. Puffs of scented smoke hang before you like phantom fruit. When Americans see the Cuban cigars in the room-sized humidor, they look like children in a sweet shop.

Cuban cigars are made from whole leaves. Dutch cigars, like Hajenius' own brand, are made of chopped blends of tobaccos: Brazilian for sweetness, Cuban for strength and Sumatran for smoothness. A map of the plantations

of Sumatra hangs like a chart of Bordeaux vineyards on the wall of the shop's cigar library.

Hajenius was started by 20-year-old Pantaleon Gerhard, who came from East Holland to Amsterdam and took two rooms in a hotel: one for living in and one for a shop. His innovation was to sell many different kinds of cigars and not just his own; an approach that forms the basis of modern retail.

The present Hajenius building has a dignified opulence. The ceiling is made of leather because paint-thinners in 1915, when the shop opened, could taint the cigars. The walls are marble pieces cut from the same slab and placed in perfect symmetry. In one room is a block of private humidors with brass nameplates. The whole shop has the measured pace of a bank: a fantasy bank where there are no desks and unlimited funds.

Right *One of the shop's cigar-smoking lessons, which instruct beginners on the finer points of blazing – or rather, how to smoke and not to blaze. The secret is to keep the cigar at the right temperature: not too hot and not too cool.*

CASA ANTIGUA

Ceramics

FOUNDED 1904, *by Antonio Arjona*

OWNER *Fernando Arjona, the third generation*

SPECIALITIES *Hand-made and hand-painted ceramics from all over Spain*

ADDRESS/PHONE *Isabel la Catolica 2, Madrid, Spain*

NEAR *Metro Santo Domingo*

MAIL ORDER *Shipping can be arranged*

OPENING HOURS *Monday to Friday 10am– 1.30pm, 5pm–8pm; Saturday 10am–1.30pm*

'We are a co-operative with 22 families,' owner Fernando Arjona explains. 'My grandfather dealt with their grandfathers.' Fernando's voice rises and falls in little swoops, like a bird. Custodian of this most fragile of shops, he opens the door personally and follows customers around to illuminate and darken extra chambers hidden behind curtains.

The ceramics at Casa Antigua are all hand-made and hand-painted. As a benchmark, Fernando keeps a single mass-produced tile, which he calls 'a factory souvenir'; look at it alone and the colours are bright, but when viewed against authentic craftwork it is garish, crude and mechanistic.

The personal care that is taken over each piece of pottery is reflected in the prices, not because they are high – a beautifully made mug is under £4 – but because two mugs of an almost identical design may vary in price if the artisan took 15 minutes longer to do a slightly more complex bit of work or to add a different glaze.

The designs range from the primitive expressiveness of the 10th century through the elegant geometric patterns that stem from the Moorish occupation of Spain to the twirls and curls of the 18th century. Some are more figurative, such as birds with perky struts and flourishes of flowers and leaves. Regional styles may alter from town to town and workshop to workshop.

Fernando adds that, over the years, the number of small workshops making ceramics has fallen. Some of the younger generation who went away to university no longer want to be craftworkers.

The exterior of the shop is covered in antique tiles; the interior is a three-dimensional mosaic of china. The only space not filled with ceramics – the ceiling – is covered in yellowing tourism posters from the Twenties and Thirties. Even the floor is partially tiled, apart from a blank pathway near the entrance, worn down during the decades when people had metal soles to make their shoes last longer.

GIULIO GIANNINI E FIGLIO

Stationery & bookbinding

FOUNDED 1856 by Pietro Giannini

OWNERS Brothers Enrico, Gabriele and Guido Giannini, the fifth generation

SPECIALITIES Bookbinding, marbled paper, paper-covered desk accessories

ADDRESS/PHONE Piazza Pitti 37-r, 50125 Florence, Italy; tel: (00 39) 055 212 621, fax: (00 39) 055 288 329

E-MAIL giannini@softconsulting.it

NEAR The Pitti Palace; the Ponte Vecchio

MAIL ORDER A restricted catalogue is available

OPENING HOURS Monday to Saturday 9.30am–7.30pm; closed Mondays from November to March

Giulio Giannini existed as a simple stationers until Florence became capital of Italy for several years, and the king and his court moved to the nearby Pitti Palace. Pietro Giannini, like any good trader, moved with the times and learned how to bind books, decorating the covers with gold. His son, Guido Giannini, became so adept at this new trade that he was known among Florentine artisans as the 'King of Gold'.

By this time there was another kind of customer, for the English love affair with Tuscany and Florence had begun. A photograph taken in 1904 shows the shop front covered in English advertisements designed to attract this rich source of income. When Queen Victoria visited the city (she never went to either Venice or Rome), the English

Left *The interior of this famous stationery and desk accessory shop, opposite the Pitti Palace in Florence.*

Right *One of the books kept in a safe at the back of the Giannini's. The safe contains the gems of each generation's fine bookbinding. Each mark on the embossed leather was painstakingly made by hand.*

Below *Enrico Giannini making marbled paper.*

community in Tuscany commissioned Giannini's to make a special photograph album as a memento for the monarch. It was at this time that the so-called Florentine style was born, with the neo-Gothic spikes and scrolls revealing the influence of Victorian tastes on local style. This still sells today, although one of the current owners, Enrico Giannini, says it is far from being his personal favourite – too fussy.

Times were hard after the First World War, and Giannini's, looking for cheaper products, struck upon the idea of covering books and desk accessories not with leather but with paper. This is the style for which the shop is famous.

There are small, imaginative presents for around £5 that you can tuck in a suitcase, sheets of hand-marbled paper and well-crafted objects such as address books, all tailored for the modern times of tourism. But the heart of the business is still fine bookbinding, something you would not know from a casual browse in the shop.

The workshop upstairs houses a collection of 3,500 tools, all still in use today, for embossing the leather bindings with gold motifs derived from every style from Medieval and Renaissance to art deco designs. A wood-covered safe contains precious examples of work, and each generation of the family has a shelf of its own.

Enrico Giannini remembers how, at the age of ten, he learned to decorate simple bookmarks and fill in hand-painted cards alongside his grandmother, a skilled calligrapher who worked anonymously because it was not considered fitting for a woman. 'You start to learn when you are still playing and you don't realize you've started to learn the work,' he says.

Gilding is painstaking work. The little tools are heated in a gas flame and must be exactly the right temperature to make the gold stick to the leather. Each impression must be done with a concentrated attention; nothing is mechanical. A specialist trade such as this is dependent upon other small businesses that are themselves changing. Leather, for example, used to be tanned for months using bark; now it is done more quickly with chemicals, leaving a sheen and lack of elasticity that mean it is much more difficult to make an impression with the embossing tools. They must form alliances with other traditional craftworkers so that they can all survive.

Enrico and his brother Guido scour flea markets for old books and boxes with old designs, which they use for inspiration. And after the terrible flood of Florence in 1961, hundreds of hand-written record books were almost ruined by the mud and water. But Giannini's saved what remained and used the old manuscripts to cover books and boxes. Thus it is they move forward while looking back.

BETHGE

Stationery

FOUNDED *In 1977 by Waltraud Bethge; the first shop was opened in 1984 by Waltraud Bethge and Vera Marisa Schober. The flagship store, featured here, opened in 1989, and another branch will be opened in Munich.*

OWNERS *Waltraud Bethge and Vera Marisa Schober*

SPECIALITIES *Customized and hand-printed stationery, a superb selection of fountain-pens, well-designed desk accessories, screen-printed wrapping paper and greeting cards*

ADDRESS *ABC Strasse 9, Hohe Bleichen, 20345 Hamburg, Germany; tel: (00 49) 40 311 551, fax: (00 49) 40 315 444*

NEAR *U-Bahn Gänsemarkt*

MAIL ORDER *A catalogue is produced every January*

OPENING HOURS *Monday to Friday 10.30am–7pm; Saturday 10.30am–4pm*

Set up to bring modern design to the traditional world of fine stationery, Bethge even sells a sexy paperclip. The clips are modernist metal curls produced by just one machine where they come out one by one: toc-toc.

Originally a graphic designer, Waltraud Bethge started the business by producing customized business cards that were screen-printed instead of embossed to allow a greater range of colour and design. Many people want business cards to look old-fashioned, and thus to buy a look that says 'years of experience'. Bethge has leapfrogged this concept by being unashamedly modern and dynamic.

Below *This modern, stylish stationery shop is in one of the smartest shopping streets in Hamburg: the ABC Strasse.*

The success of the shop proves that it may well be outsiders, with their different perspectives and wide-awake eyes, who reinvigorate tradition. Bethge's inks are non-toxic and come with names like lipsticks: soft rose, opera red, moonglow and aubergine. The metal desk accessories transform tape dispensers and hole-punches into objects of desire. One personal organizer has a cover made of stingray skin that looks like caviar, its design inspired by a 1930s' handbag.

The entire shop is as well-considered as its parts. Some stationery outlets play the rainbow game rather crudely; Bethge has just enough of this season's colours, changing in Spring and Autumn, like clothing fashions.

It also stocks design classics such as glass tube pens that work by capillary action, and a Japanese 'stapler' that cuts and folds pieces of paper together in one movement so that no staples are needed. A customer once asked if she was able to buy refills.

LEGATORIA PIAZZESI

Craft papers

FOUNDED *1900 by Carlo Bandini; taken over and renamed by Carlo Piazzesi in 1905*

OWNER *Lavinia Rizzi Carlson*

SPECIALITIES *Hand-printed paper, paper-covered stationery and objects, papier mâché*

ADDRESS/PHONE *San Marco, Santa Maria del Giglio, 2511 Venice, Italy; tel: (00 39) 041 522 1202, fax: (00 39) 041 871 8621*

E-MAIL/INTERNET *olavi@tin.it www.skyport.com/nordest/piazzesi*

NEAR *Santa Maria del Giglio; Ponte dell'Accademia; on San Marco*

OPENING HOURS *Monday to Saturday 10am–12.30pm and 4pm–7pm*

'This area used to be full of artisans' historical shops,' says Lavinia Rizzi Carlson in an ever-accelerating crescendo. 'It was full of people who loved their work. They have sold up because they couldn't face the Italian laws. Venice is becoming a big mall of big names and we are dying.' Lavinia's shop, Legatoria Piazzesi, is one of the most famous and cherished in Venice; yet its future hangs in the balance.

At the time of writing, Lavinia was considering turning the shop into a showroom open mostly by appointment. There were a number of reasons for this: the myriad new taxes and laws were particularly burdensome on small businesses; meddling bureaucrats walked into the shop six times a month interfering in such issues as prices; and

Left *The exterior
of this unique paper
shop, with the
reflection of a
Venetian bridge in
the front window.*

Right *The shop sells
papers using many
different craft
printing techniques,
including patterns
taken originally from
the curtains of old
monasteries.*

copyrighted designs had been ripped off.
A published poet and a psychoanalyst
before becoming a shopkeeper, Lavinia
was used to a more contemplative life.
She had just come back from holiday to
a stack of brown envelopes and problems.

Legatoria sells attractive craft papers,
which are made using 13 different
techniques. Some are patterned with
wood blocks originally used to print on
cloth. The subtle colours and shapes are
reminiscent of the printing techniques
of the Far East, and a reminder of the
fact that Venice grew as a trading nation.

Above all, Lavinia would like to keep
such traditional crafts going. It is in
her blood: the fine paper business that
her great-grandfather set up has long
supplied Legatoria Piazzesi (this was part
of the reason why she bought the shop).

The shop may yet remain open, or
the workshop will continue, with sales
conducted via a showroom. Is this the
future of small craft businesses, visited
by those in-the-know but hidden from
the passerby? And will this beautiful
place become yet another international
designer-label shop?

THE CREATIVE SPIRIT

L CORNELISSEN & SON

Artists' materials

FOUNDED *1854 by Louis Dieudonne Cornelissen*

OWNER *Nicholas Walt*

SPECIALITIES *Supplier of materials for painters, gilders and printmakers*

ADDRESS/PHONE *105 Great Russell Street, London WC1B 3RY; tel: 020 7636 1045, fax: 020 7636 3655*

INTERNET *www.cornelissen.com*

NEAR *The British Museum; Tottenham Court Road Underground; J M Smith's umbrella shop (see pages 116–117)*

MAIL ORDER *Worldwide service, £1.50 handling charge*

OPENING HOURS *Monday to Friday 9.30am–5.30pm; Saturday 9.30am–5pm*

Above *A missionary leaving the shop. He had come in for special nibs for calligraphy. The shop gets many religious artists as customers, often after pigments for icons.*

Right *Some of the jars of pure pigment that form a wall of colour on the left side of the shop. Cornelissen's use around 37 suppliers for the pigments alone.*

Cornelissen delights and informs both the curious and the craftsperson. First of all, it is a visual feast. One wall of the Victorian interior is lined with jars of pure pigment: pinks and oranges, earthy umbers and ochres, the deep brilliance of crimsons and blues, five whites and seven blacks. At the back of the shop are plain, inch-high wooden drawers, which pull back quietly to reveal 2,000 dazzling shades of pastel. It makes you realize that, despite their trade, and customers, other artists' suppliers are visually rather dull.

For all this beauty, Cornelissen's charm lies in its artisanal, down-to-earth usefulness. Artists and craftworkers come here for the materials and tools of their trades. 'We like to think of ourselves as a plumbers' merchant,' says owner Nicholas Walt. Together with a Greek icon restorer, Nicholas rescued the business when the founding family died out in 1978 and is obsessed, in the most intelligent sense of the word, with artists' materials. Nearly every sale involves a conversation, and customers overhear such fascinating snippets as why the best brushes are made from the tails of male sables – particularly when they are extra-lustrous thanks to the exercise of foraging for their young in the winter months.

Cornelissen's serves anyone and everyone: students at the nearby Slade, Central and St Martin's art schools; weekend watercolourists; major artists such as Lucian Freud, Bridget Riley and Howard Hodgkin. Gilders choose from 30 kinds of genuine gold leaf for frames, walls, furniture – even for food and hairdressing. Nuns come in for small jars of pigment for icons. Interior designers buy in bulk to make staggering hues to cover walls.

In the basement of the shop are further treasures, such as a jar of the rare, translucently beautiful Genuine

Indian Yellow pigment, made many years ago by feeding cows with mango leaves and collecting the earth that has mixed with their acidic urine. This and other rare objects are to go on permanent display, adding yet another dimension to this remarkable place.

Pigment, says Nicholas Walt, is the quintessence of colour. The earthy hues tend to come from the soils of Cyprus and Italy, the metal-derived cadmiums from England. The shop grinds down lapis lazuli for a blue you could fly through. When the maker of manganese blue threatened to stop producing it, Cornelissen and other members of what Nicholas calls 'the pigment-freak network' banded together to keep it going. The shop also sell the glass mullers that are used to mix pure pigment with linseed or poppy oil to make oil paints, with egg yolk to make tempura, and with gum arabic to make watercolours.

Left *Some of the 2,000 pastels that are stored in slim drawers at the back of the shop.*

Right *A French watercolour chart from the Lefranc company, which dates back to the late-19th century. It would have been put up in a shop to show off the company's colour range.*

Cornelissen commissions or makes other objects such as gilders' cushions and sketchbooks of whatever paper you choose, and works with a fletcher who makes flights for arrows and also prepares the feathers for Cornelissen's quills. Nicholas would not disclose his name: 'A shop like this has secrets.'

Many of Cornelissen's transactions are time-consuming and painstaking; customers often have very specific requirements, and for each purchase there are often several technical questions. And you realize that a shop like this – with its depth of knowledge and contacts – is, in many ways, much more than just a shop.

Right *Some of the goods on sale are kept in beautiful glass jars like this. 'Nearly everything we buy must have something done to it before it is sold,' says Nicholas Walt.*

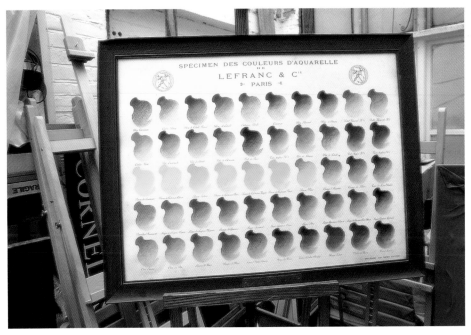

LAMBIEK

Comic strips

FOUNDED *1968 by Kees Kousemaker*

OWNER *Kees Kousemaker*

SPECIALITIES *New and classic comic strips*

ADDRESS/PHONE *Kerkstraat 78, 1017 GN Amsterdam, Netherlands; tel: (00 31) 20 626 7543, fax: (00 31) 20 620 6372*

E-MAIL/INTERNET *lambiek@lambiek www.lambiek.net.nlcom*

NEAR *The Rijksmuseum (about seven minutes' walk)*

MAIL ORDER *No catalogue, but the shops tries to have 'everything worthwhile' and will send orders around the world*

OPENING HOURS *Monday to Friday 10.30am–6pm; Saturday 10.30am–5pm; Sunday 12noon–4pm*

Right *Lambiek is one of the oldest specialist comic shops to be found in Europe, first opening for business in 1968*

At first glance, Lambiek has an engagingly ramshackle air. People drop by for a chat and a cup of tea with the owner, Kees Kousemaker, who sits like a benevolently observant host near the till whilst customers of all ages sift through his vast mass of comics, as if hunting for buried gold in a paper flea-market. Soon you discover that the shelves are efficiently arranged by alphabet and that the shop, in fact, holds an impressive, capacious collection of comics, including some which are now extremely valuable. Strips that sold originally for 35 cents can be worth thousands of dollars 30 years on.

The whole comic-strip world has changed radically since Kees set up the shop in 1968, as part of the Amsterdam counterculture that took a delight in youth culture and challenged the accepted hierarchies of 'Art'. Kees opened up in a basement where he had to spread out the comics to make his new shop seem full. Lambiek was such a success that he eventually moved up in the world: to ground-floor premises.

Vintage comics have grown in value and early *Superman* comics now soar in price in Internet auctions. Kees does not deal in this fly-away end of the market but tries to sell everything that he considers to be worthwhile in artistic terms. *Tintin* and erotic strips are the shop's money-spinners.

The shop retains an edge. If an unestablished artist produces just 20 hand-made booklets, four of them might end up here. Lambiek also has a gallery space to display works, often rejected by the art establishment, that occupy an undefined area between graphic and 'fine' art.

The Dutch, like the British, are lucky to share a language with a country that is renowned for its cartoons: what the United States is to Britain, Belgium is to Holland. In all, Lambiek stocks strips in 20 languages. Most languages seem to be tongue-tied in one respect: the English terms 'comic strip' and 'cartoon' do not get close to conveying the vast and varied range of graphic literature available at Lambiek.

Above and below *At Lambiek, Kees Kousemaker stocks everything from innocent Disney comics to the type of erotica that points back to the shop's roots as a centre of counterculture.*

SAUTTER + LACKMANN

Arts books

FOUNDED *1970, by Hinrich and Gisela Sautter and Dierk Lackmann*

OWNER *Hinrich Sautter*

SPECIALITIES *Books about fine arts, decorative arts, photography, film, design and architecture*

ADDRESS *Admiralitätstrasse 71–72, 20459 Hamburg, Germany; tel: (00 49) 40 373 196, fax: (00 49) 40 365 479*

E-MAIL *BH-Sautter@t-online.de*

NEAR *U-Bahn Rödingsmarkt*

MAIL ORDER *Catalogue available; will also send books on other subjects published in Germany as an additional service*

OPENING HOURS *Monday to Friday 10am–6.30pm; Saturday 10am–4pm*

Above *The bookshelves at Sautter + Lackmann have been designed to hold books that are nearly all 'out-size'.*

The best bookshops have the feel of personal libraries. Sautter + Lackmann is mostly silent, apart from turning pages and the erratic creaks of floorboards as browsers – static as stalagmites – absorb the drip, drip, drip of words. The motion is internal: in one aisle an electric-blue-toenailed designer visualises costumes for a film, in another an architect builds an idea in his head.

You can travel through worlds here, from neon to Velázquez, to gardening, to a discourse on yellow, to a whole section on paperweights, to a whole room on photography. All the shelves are tall in order to fit in 35,000 titles, and many of the books themselves are works of art. There is even a book on the aesthetics of art books.

It is no surprise to find a specialist shop such as this in Germany, where the book trade is strong at all levels. A two-year apprenticeship for booksellers helps foster a professional pride in showing that they can get whatever the customer wants in any subject. Many publishing companies still retain an area of specialization; perhaps not just theology, but Christianity, and then Catholicism rather than Protestantism.

Owner Hinrich Sautter wants this shop to be comprehensive in its field. When it transpired there were no books on Portuguese tiles in German, he stocked one in Portuguese. Sometimes the staff complains about the books that will not shift, and Hinrich tells them of the delight of an Australian friend when he came across a book on Australian barns he had been searching for in his own country for ten years.

Customers might come in and ask about an interesting painter who captured their eye in a gallery. Hinrich swoops down from his book-lined nest, looks over his glasses and paces the shelves on a quest. 'The joy of specializing is that it never ends,' he says. 'There is a horizon, and you go a long way towards it but you never get there. You are challenged again and again, and the challenge is what makes it interesting.'

Above and left
The shop is a house of books where readers spend hours browsing. There is a table and rocking chair at the back for long-term browsers, as well as a little rocking horse for children.

JOHN SANDOE

Books

FOUNDED *1957 by John Sandoe*

OWNERS *John de Falbe, Seán Jackson
and Stewart Grimshaw*

SPECIALITIES *An intelligent, inspired
selection of books*

ADDRESS/PHONE *10 Blacklands Terrace,
Chelsea, London SW3 2SR; tel: 020 7589
9473, fax: 020 7581 2084*

E-MAIL/INTERNET
*books@jsandoe.demon.co.uk
www.johnsandoe.com*

MAIL ORDER *Books sent for the cost of the
postage; quarterly catalogue of new books*

NEAR *Sloane Square Underground;
V V Rouleaux ribbon shop (see pages 104–105)*

OPENING HOURS *Monday to Saturday
9.30am–5.30pm; Wednesday 9.30am–7.30pm*

'In certain respects I know my customers
better than their spouses do,' said John
de Falbe, co-owner of one of the best
bookshops in Britain. 'It's like dropping
an archaeological shaft into somebody;
you go a short way into many layers
through the books that they like.'
He was sitting in the one room with
space for a speck of dust. Elsewhere,
books climbed the stairs, crept along
the floor, filled my entire vision.

Crowded, yes, but John Sandoe's
still manages to stock favourite books
in hardback, no matter if they are
current bestsellers or not, and they
have invented a system of sliding
shelves, which were copied by the
architect Norman Foster, to display
the paperback fiction by front cover
rather than spine.

Right *Books fill every corner of this exceptional shop. John Sandoe's selection of stock is governed by the principle of 'sheer prejudice', says one owner, John de Falbe.*

Left *Tucked away just off the King's Road, John Sandoe may be small but it somehow contains many of the interesting books that far larger shops fail to stock.*

The staff, who are often writers and former customers, build up sections with judgement and pleasure. (One of the owners, a Joycean, keeps an extra stash upstairs.) If you want informed guidance, they invariably display an encyclopaedic knowledge of the stock, and are not afraid to be partisan. It is one of the few bookshops where you may be actively discouraged from buying one book in preference for another.

I went through the shop from section to section, halted and diverted by odd juxtapositions. Primo Levi passed me on to Carl Hiaassen; Talleyrand, somehow, stood shoulder to shoulder with Martin Amis. London doorways led to salmon fishing in Russia. As I browsed, a famous playwright walked into the shop asking rapid questions on three different subjects. Then he went out to look at the boot of his large car, as if to check it were large enough. Later, someone told me he wrote for two weeks of the year and otherwise read a great deal. Only the famous playwright knows the truth of this story, but here, it certainly seems possible.

GELBE MUSIK

Modern music

FOUNDED *1981 by Ursula Block*
OWNER *Ursula Block*
SPECIALITIES *Modern music: artist's records, phonetic poetry, early avant-garde, electronic, futurism, industrial, minimal; exhibitions four times a year*
ADDRESS *Schaperstrasse 11, D-10719 Berlin,*
Germany; tel: (00 49) 30 211 39 62, fax: (00 49) 30 217 64 32
NEAR *Augsburger Strasse U-Bahn 15; Spichernstrasse and Kufürstendamm U-Bahn 9 and 15*
MAIL ORDER *Catalogue available*
OPENING HOURS *Tuesday–Friday 1pm–6pm; Saturday 11am–2pm*

Left *Gelbe Musik is situated in a quiet street in the area frequented in the Thirties by the English writer Christopher Isherwood.*

Right *The interior is a cross between minimalist space, art gallery and shop. Ursula's dog, Luzie, seen here, could be better known as His Mistress' Voice.*

Gelbe Musik's mail-order list is full of the international avant-garde. The members of the influential group Kraftwerk are friends; DJs drop by for new sounds. The week I visited, a young Russian had been coming in every day to find recordings of futurist music that had been made in his own country.

When you walk into Gelbe Musik, there is an impression of space and light, that this is a cross between art gallery and music shop. 'It used to be minimalist,' says owner and curator Ursula Block. She set up the shop in order to display the cross-over between visual and aural art and has built up an archive of avant-garde music in the back room. The shop's name, which means 'Yellow Music', is the title of a musical work by Kandinsky. The sounds on offer range from Tom Waits and Brian Eno to John Cage, Stockhausen to the likes of 'red deer rutting'.

Ursula puts on a recording of an artist who has taken records of musicians such as Louis Armstrong and Johann Strauss and physically played with the discs as they spun. As the music begins to sound like the growling yawn of a lion, Ursula's dog, Luzie, starts to bark at the speakers.

Left *Many of the CD sleeves are art works in themselves, and are consequently displayed in full view. Gelbe Musik also holds specific exhibitions four times a year.*

SHOPPING LISTS

SHOPS BY COUNTRY

AUSTRIA

GEGENBAUER
Pages 34–37
Vinegars & pickled vegetables
Waldgasse 3, Vienna
tel: (00 43) 1 6041 0880

BELGIUM

AU GRAND RASOIR
Pages 86–87
Blades
7 rue de l'Hôpital, Brussels
tel: (00 32) 2 512 49 62

BEER MANIA
Pages 48–49
Belgian beer
Chaussée de Wavre 174–176, Brussels
tel: (00 32) 2 512 1788

WITTAMER
Pages 58–59
Cakes
6-12-13 Place du Grand Sablon, Brussels
tel: (00 32) 2 512 37 42

CZECH REPUBLIC

BRIC-A-BRAC 1 AND BRIC-A-BRAC 2
Pages 100–103
Art deco objects and bric-à-brac
Tynsk 7, Prague
Bric-à-Brac 1 tel: (00 42 0) 2 232 6484
Bric-à-Brac 2 tel: (00 42 0) 2 248 15763

FRANCE

DEYROLLE
Pages 72–73
Taxidermy & natural history
46 rue du Bac, Paris
tel: (00 33) 1 42 22 30 07

LEGRAND FILLES & FILS
Pages 46–47
Wine
1 rue de la Banque, Paris
tel: (00 33) 1 42 60 07 12

LA MAISON DU MIEL
Pages 56–57
Honey
24 rue Vignon, Paris
tel: (00 33) 1 47 42 26 70

LIONEL POILANE
Pages 20–23
Bread
8 rue du Cherche-Midi, Paris
tel: (00 33) 1 45 48 42 59

M G W SEGAS
Pages 108–111
Canes
34 Passage Jouffroy, Paris
tel: (00 33) 1 47 70 89 65

GERMANY

BETHGE
Pages 132–133
Staitonery
ABC-Strasse 9, Hamburg
tel: (00 49) 40 311 551

GELBE MUSIK
Pages 148–149
Modern music
Schaperstrasse 11, Berlin
tel: (00 49) 30 211 39 62

HOLZAPFEL
Pages 74–75
Tools
Kollwitzstrasse 100, Berlin
tel: (00 49) 30 4405 2004

DIE IMAGINARE MANUFAKTUR
Pages 66–67
Brushes & brooms
Oranienstrasse 26, Berlin
tel: (00 49) 30 2588 6614

KNOPF PAUL
Pages 112–113
Buttons
Zossener Strasse 10, Berlin
tel: (00 49) 30 692 1212

PFUND'S MOLKEREI
Pages 26–27
Cheese
Bautzner Strasse 79, Dresden
tel: (00 49) 35 180 8080

SAUTTER + LACKMANN
Pages 144–145
Arts books
Admiralitätstrasse 71–72, Hamburg
tel: (00 49) 40 373 196

GREAT BRITAIN
BERRY BROS & RUDD
Pages 42–45
Wine
3 St James's Street, London
tel: 020 7396 9669

JAMES BOWDEN AND WEBBER & SONS
Pages 80–81
Hardware shops
The Square, Chagford
tel: 01647 433271

L CORNELISSEN & SON
Pages 138–141
Artists' materials
105 Great Russell Street, London
tel: 020 7636 1045

ROBERT CRESSER
Pages 64–65
Brushes & brooms
40 Victoria Street, Edinburgh
tel: 0131 225 2181

LARCH COTTAGE NURSERIES
Pages 90–93
Plants & pizzas
Melkinthorpe, Penrith
tel: 01931 712404

ROBERT MILLS, ARCHITECTURAL ANTIQUES
Pages 68–71
Architectural salvage
Narroways Road, Eastville, Bristol
tel: 0117 955 6542

V V ROULEAUX
Pages 104–105
Ribbons
54 Sloane Square, London
tel: 020 7730 3125

J M SMITH & SONS
Pages 116–117
Umbrellas & sticks
Hazelwood House, 53 New Oxford Street,
London
tel: 020 7836 4731

POLLOCK'S TOY MUSEUM
Pages 84–85
Toy theatres & toys
1 Scala Street, London
tel: 020 7636 3452

JOHN SANDOE
Pages 146–147
Books
10 Blacklands Terrace, London
tel: 020 7589 9473

VALVONA & CROLLA
Pages 14–17
Delicatessen
19 Elm Row, Edinburgh
tel: 0131 556 6066

ITALY
PAOLO BRANDOLISIO
Pages 76–77
Gondola oar locks
Castello 4725, Venice
tel: (00 39) 041 522 4155

IL GELATO DI SAN CRISPINO
Pages 54–55
Ice-cream
Via Panetteria 42, Rome
tel: (00 39) 06 679 3924

GIULIO GIANNINI E FIGLIO
Pages 128–131)
Stationery & bookbinding
Piazza Pitti 37-r, Florence
tel: (00 39) 055 212 621

LEGATORIA PIAZZESI
Pages 134–135
Craft papers
San Marco, Santa Maria del Giglio, Venice
tel: (00 39) 041 522 1202

PHARMACEUTICA DI SANTA MARIA NOVELLI
Pages 98–99
Perfumes and toileteries
Via della Scala 16n, Florence
tel: (00 39) 055 230 2883/2649/2437

TAMBURINI
Pages 28–29
Delicatessen
Via Caprarie 1, Bologna
tel: (00 39) 051 234 726

TADDEI
Pages 122–123
Leather boxes
Via Santa Margherita 11, Florence
tel: (00 39) 055 239 8960

NETHERLANDS
BRILMUSEUM
Pages 96–97
Spectacles
Gasthuismolensteeg 7, Amsterdam
tel: (00 31) 20 421 2414

P G J HAJENIUS
Pages 124–125
Cigars and pipes
Rokin 92–96, Amsterdam
tel: (00 31) 20 623 7494

JACOB HOOY
Pages 32–33
Herbs & spices
Kloveniersburgwal 12, Amsterdam
tel: (00 31) 20 624 3041

LAMBIEK
Pages 142–143
Comic strips
Kerkstraat 78, Amsterdam
tel: (00 31) 20 626 7543

T'MANNETJE
Pages 82–83
Bicycles
Frans Halsstraat 26A, Amsterdam
(00 31) 20 679 2139

DE TAART VAN M'N TANTE
Pages 60–61
Modern cakes
Eerste Jacob van Campenstraat 35,
Amsterdam
tel: (00 31) 20 776 4600

SPAIN

CASA ANTIGUA
Pages 126–127
Ceramics
Isabel la Catolica 2, Madrid
tel: (00 34) 91 547 3417

CASA CRESPO
Pages 106–107
Espadrilles
Calle del Divino Pastor 29, Madrid
tel: (00 34) 91 521 5654

ESCRIBA
Pages 52–53
Cakes & chocolates
Rambla de les Flors 83, Barcelona
tel: (00 34) 93 301 6027

E & A GISPERT
Pages 18–19
Toasted nuts & dried fruits
Sombrerers 23, Barcelona
tel: (00 34) 93 319 7535

HERBORISTERIA DEL REI
Pages 114–115
Herbal pharmacy
Carrer del Vidre 1, Barcelona
tel: (00 34) 93 318 0512

EL REY DE LA MAGIA
Pages 88–89
Magic
Carrer Princesa 11, Barcelona
tel: (00 34) 93 319 7393

SWEDEN

MARIANNE'S FISK OCH DELIKATESSEN
Pages 24–25
Delicatessen
Karlbergsvägen 67, Stokholm
tel: (00 46) 8 30 10 71

LJUNGGRENS PAPPERSHANDEL
Pages 120–121
Paper
Suartmangatan 9, Stokholm
tel: (00 46) 8 676 0383

PLASTEN
Pages 78–79
Plastic
St Eriksgata 70, Stokholm
tel: (00 46) 8 341 650

ROSENDALS TRADGARD
Pages 30–31
Fruit & vegetables
Rosendalsterrassen 12, Stokholm
tel: (00 46) 8 545 81270

SIBYLLANS COFFEE AND TEA SHOP
Pages 40–41
Coffee & tea
Sibyllegatan 35, Stokholm
tel: (00 46) 8 662 0663

INDEX

ACKNOWLEDGEMENTS

I would like to thank those who generously gave me hospitality and
company on my travels, or who pointed me in the direction of interesting
shops, particularly Anette Dieng, Sophie Kidd, Diana Henry, Mark Diaper,
Birgit Eggers, Ivan Day, Johnny Ray, Vickie Mackenzie, Alex Ellis and
Teresa Adegas, Jibba in Prague, and Katrin and Irene at Nikolai in Berlin.
I would like to offer a heart-felt thanks to Jenny Linford for giving me a
great head-start on the list, the commissioning editor, Margaret Little, for
sushi and support, and Steve Guise and Tracy Killick at Mitchell Beazley.
Most of all, I would like to thank the owners of these exceptional shops
for taking the time to talk to me, and the photographer, Jill Mead, who,
besides being comitted and talented, was more than a joy to work with.
She always managed, somehow, to go the extra distance.

This book is dedicated to Jill and to Gordon.